TAMIA A. MCEWEN, PHD

MIND AS WELL

A Journey from Discovery to Recovery and Beyond

Mind as Well

Mind as Well:
A Journey from Discovery to Recovery and Beyond

Tamia A. McEwen, PhD

ISBN: 978-1-7363731-1-8
Printed Version

Cover Photo: Courtesy of Errol George

DEDICATION

This book is dedicated to the peer community, Black girls, and people everywhere who could not feel the sunshine and wondered if they were enough. You are enough. You do matter. You belong here. Take up space.
Love, Tamia

TABLE OF CONTENTS

MESSAGES OF LOVE

The vision for this book is a full circle view and offering of my life experiences in phases: The Journey discusses my family network and inherited connections; Discovery contains the onset of mental illness, initial diagnosis, responding to stress and learning the impact of conflict, and boundary setting; Recovery includes navigating the mental health sector as a person served and professional while defining wellness for myself and dealing with the physical onset of uterine fibroid tumors; Beyond covers moving into advocacy first within myself and then by sharing my lived experiences, stepping into healing through lifestyle as wellness support that includes all dimensions. *Mind as Well* inspires by releasing shame, seeing all parts of me (present, past, and those to come) as well no matter the condition, and it explores connecting with the human experience of just being. I hope you enjoy the read and the journey.

Love,

Tamia

A Cousin's Companionship

Brava my dear cousin Tamia! I have no doubt that this book will inspire, heal, and encourage many to walk their own wellness journey with grace and confidence.

Dr. Tamia McEwen has delivered a raw and positively vulnerable account of her mental health journey in *Mind as Well*. As a Licensed Clinical Psychologist, I see many clients that have internal barriers toward behavioral change. A major hurdle that often revolts against emotional wellness is internalized shaming resulting in feeling alone and sometimes defeated. Tamia has conquered this mountain in her personal and captivating narrative of her discovery and recovery from stigma and shaming. There is so much information in this easy yet dense read. I know I increased my knowledge and gained a new perspective. The short stories and poetry take my emotions on a joyous rollercoaster ride with humor, sadness, frustration, love and so much more. Tamia, your gift of truth telling, and creative pen has me excited to take more risks in my own relationships and live out loud a bit more. I know your journey isn't easy, but your shine is so bright, and your swag is everything.

---Lovingly, Deidre Ann Weathersby, Ph.D.

A Mother's Love

On August 16th, 1974 I called my mom and asked her why I kept going to the bathroom. She laughed as I explained that I was constantly going to the bathroom. I can still hear her voice clearly and distinctly. "Girl your water broke, and you are in labor! Get to the hospital! And where is Elton?" I hung up as Elton walked in with the news that we could drive to the hospital in our newly purchased car. Tamia was delivered a couple of hours later. My name is Beatrice L. Jokines, and the author of this book is Dr. Tamia A. McEwen, my daughter.

Tamia has so many defining moments in her journey, and I am so glad she has decided to share her story with everyone. She's always kept a journal and shared some of her writings, short stories, poems and prose with me. I've witnessed her triumphs and her stumbles and her resilience...through it all, never giving up her faith. She has made me more aware of the important connection food, exercise, meditation and breath have as medicine to overall physical and mental health. Her determination and belief that we can all be well is supported by research and accreditation from medical journals. She presents it so well you don't realize its complexities. Her writing is so spell bounding.

I believe everyone afforded the opportunity to read this book will find a fresh, thought provoking look at the struggles as told by someone who is a living testimony in overcoming mental health issues. It will keep you engaged as you become informed and amazed all at once.

I still look at you in amazement, you are such a bright light. Congratulations daughter!

---Beatrice L. Jokines

"Soror Mommy"

Mind as Well

INTRODUCTION

HEART WORK

During a prayer session at church one Sunday morning, a pastor prayed and whispered close to my ear, "Lord heal her heart." I had gotten in the Intercessory Prayer Line for no specific reason. I just knew I wanted something—whatever it was that I needed to make it along my journey, I wanted it. I was not in a relationship. In fact, I had not even been in a serious adult relationship. I was not dating. I was abstinent because I was waiting for marriage, of course. I did not see myself as a person whose heart needed mending. My mind, on the other hand, was an entirely different story. I was on the mend, the mind mend. I was 23 years old and a first-year teacher. I had just graduated from college one year prior. I was on the mend from a major, massive, public nervous breakdown. My mind had "split." That was the only way that I could describe it. Because of this breakdown, I thought something was wrong with me. I thought many things: I thought I was crazy. I thought I was mentally ill. I thought I was schizophrenic. I thought I was weird. I thought I was broken. I thought I would be alone forever. I thought no one would understand me. I thought I would never understand myself. I thought I was lost. I thought I needed healing. I thought God had abandoned me. I thought. And I thought. And I thought.

Before this complete break, I was many things and terrified was one of them. I was terrified of everything: people's perceptions, uncertainty, the possibility of embarrassment, failure, rejection. These fears formed in my heart and plagued my mind. I had private conversations that I never verbalized. Secret crushes that I never revealed. I silently hoped for love and experienced rejection all within myself; never even verbalizing these feelings to anyone; not even really admitting to myself that these thoughts and feelings were mine, that these desires were mine. These hopes, dreams and disappointments formed in my heart and plagued my mind, breaking them both at the same time. I was heartbroken and because of it, a shattered mind was soon to come.

I knew nothing about the effects of stress—chronic, toxic or otherwise. I knew nothing about my genetic composition or using nutrition to fuel my mind, body, and spirit. I knew nothing about the power of pursuing my dreams, exploring my desires and managing my stress—having a true release or outlet. All of my adolescent life I had been an athlete. My mother had the presence of mind to keep me busy. Whether or not she realized the power of that dopamine and serotonin production, I do not know. What I do know is that athletics kept me balanced while I was an adolescent. I maintained a consistently active life throughout college, though it waxed and waned a bit like the moon, with me leaning into longer hours and shorter spurts of sleep with stalled activity. When I was active, it was mainly for weight management. I knew nothing about the effects of stress or connection with nutrition to my overall functioning, moods, emotions, willpower or health. Had I known the importance of wellness, I would have taken better care of my heart thereby taking better care of myself and my mind.

What is the purpose of this memoir? It is a book of lessons learned, compiled after 43 full years lived. In year 44, it was extended with a renewed perspective of not just who I was but the life that I have lived thus far. Now, in year 46, it is a measure of completeness. It is a love letter and series of vignettes. It is a revelation and some regrets. It is research, poetry and prose in making sense of these years that I have lived. It is questions that I still have, and it is hope. It is also heartache and dreams deferred. It is the stuff that we are made of and the thread that binds us together in this single human experience as we share this planet seeking to simply do good and be well. I offered the hope that through my life, my lived experiences, we can learn all the more how to be well: mind, body, soul and emotions. Knowing that life is not happening to us, it is happening because of us, because of our purpose and we are exactly who we need to be at this moment of our lives, living not only the dream but the destiny we were meant to live, we can see our entire self as well. I offered the hope to realize that we are already well, just as we are. The only voice we need to listen to intently is the one that is within, the one that reminds us of our truest desire. There we will find ourselves. There we will find peace. There we will find the answers to every question we seek: even if that answer is stillness, silence, or better yet, more questions. For our only task is to be more of ourselves each day.

Although I may speak directly to my readers throughout this memoir, it is simply my story and how I have made sense of my life thus far, or what questions I still have. It's not a guidebook or prescription or handbook or directive. It's not even advice. As Jessamyn Stanley reminds us, "Every Body" is different. My lessons are mine, so what did or did not work for me may not work for someone else. But what it might do is shed some light, open a door, provoke some thought, or dispel a myth. I am a teacher at heart but instead of proselytizing, I would rather my entire life be the lesson where humanity can take from it what it will: keeping what resonates and leaving the rest to appreciate simply as my lived experience. If I have learned any lesson in my life journey, that would be to simply surrender into *being* instead of *doing*. I spent a large portion of my life playing roles, figuring out what my new task was supposed to look like, and matching it. I have made some great strides and achieved high honors doing such. The times that I face now call for more authenticity. They call for an intention that can only come from my own inner voice. My own soul. My own spirit. I invite others to examine theirs as well or simply appreciate the journey that I have shared. Whether or not this is some kind of awakening, I am not sure. I do know that I have chosen—I have dared to do life differently. And in doing so, I am in a space that I have never before occupied, and I am uncomfortably satisfied in this space. Enjoy the journey and remember to Be Well my friends.

Mind as Well

SEARCHING FOR MIA: AS I BREATHE

As I breathe.

I dream dreams that I never had the courage to dream.

I visualize a life for myself that I always wanted to be.

As I breathe.

I build bridges from past to present and future selves to come.

On ships I send negative thoughts across the sea of my mind and exchange them with new realities of strength and hope.

As I breathe.

I examine the parts of me that are difficult to look at but necessary: For we cannot change what we will not face.

As I breathe.

I grow stronger, even if my strength manifests in humility because a balanced being walks in harmony.

As I breathe.

My body feels stronger. My will grows louder. My head feels lighter. My patience longer.

As I breathe, I remember that I come as one, but stand as 10,000.

Dreams and visions of my ancestors are carried out through me.

I remember that I am the change I seek, so I commit to continue to breathe.

I am in fact the dream and the hope of the enslaved. The legacy of Kings and Queens—royal blood flows through my veins.

As I breathe. Through doubt and uncertainty. Through fear and even into love.

I breathe for hope. For peace. For strength. For renewal. For community. For love. For healing. For forgiveness. For courage. For clarity. For stillness. For change.

I breathe for a new vision of myself that laughs in the face of adversity and stands up to fear.

I breathe not only for the courage to change what I cannot accept, but also to embrace the stillness of not knowing whether or not things will work out the way I desire.

I breathe for the remembrance of being both created and a creator. I manifest my desire.

I breathe for the permission to want more. To be more. And to know that I am already enough.

I breathe to remind myself that I am human. To see my own reflection and say: She is good.

PART ONE:

THE JOURNEY

WHERE I'M FROM

I'm from southern cooking and big family picnics.
Two parent homes that became a single parent home
Long talks on the telephone and late nights watching TV
Church choirs and good preaching
Summers in Chicago and Spring Breaks in California
Vacations in Germany and secret talks with my sister
I'm from love and trust
I'm from freedom

I'm from Chicago. Cook County Hospital. South Side. 95th
and Avalon.
Swimming pool in backyard porch with lush green grass
by Papa's garden.
Taking chances with glances and forbidden kisses through
green fences.
The front yard and backyard as my perimeter because Big
Mama said I'm too fast.

I'm from structure and flexibility.
I'm family secrets and truth.
I'm El Paso. Dancing the Cumbia and Quinceañeras.
Bobbing for apples,
Pinning the tale on donkeys after playing "hide and go
get it" and touch football.
From cousins and aunties close like sisters and brothers,
Deacon boards and Sunday School attendance. Super
Mario and Sega Genesis,
Hopscotch drawn in driveways with the good rocks.

From playing marbles and taking the boulder with my
clear pretty one.
From scheduled fights at Kelly Park to avenge my stolen
clarinet,
And break dancing with my crew after watching Breaking
2 Electric Boogaloo.

I'm from good memories.
I'm from childhood greatness.
I'm from HBCU Pride knowing that "Prairie View
Produces Productive People".
Non-Traditional student because my learning will last a
lifetime.
Psychology #1, MEd #2, PhD in C & I make #3 letters "not
in use". MA in Reading #4, and RYT just because I wanted
more than what was before me.
Or maybe to heal the trauma that became before me. I
am from survival.

I'm from striving forward.
I'm from building legacies.
I'm from Houston young adulthood, 22 years a teacher
and 2 years a yogini.
From transitions from Texas to Florida with the sun on
my back in two states.
From molding young minds to building bridges to Be Well
Friends.
From 20 pearls and Ivies.
From heart openers.
From peace.
From love.

2

INHERITANCE

One of the greatest gifts that a parent can give a child is a sense of purpose. As human beings we are constantly seeking to find our "place in the world". Many of us engage in various acts all to answer the universal question of "Who am I? What is my purpose?" Oddly enough, if we do not determine for ourselves who we are and what our purpose is, someone or something else most certainly will.

I never felt like I fit snuggly anywhere. My earliest recollections are of traveling, visiting. Visiting family in Chicago. Visiting family in Louisiana. Visiting family in Mississippi. Visiting friends. Spending the night at a friend's house or family member's house. Visiting. An outsider. An outside child.

You're not from here, are you?

You talk funny. Where are you from?

That was that question that stumped me every time. Where are you from? Well, shit. It depends on how you look at it, what you're asking or what you really want to know. I'm from a lot of places. I found myself rehearsing what I would say to people the next time someone asked me that question. It was uncomfortable because it was complicated as hell, depending on how you looked at it. And I could also see the annoyance on people's faces when my explanation exceeded the amount of time they were willing to give me to explain, where I was from. "Why is she still talking? It's a simple question. Where are you from?" But that's just it. Where I'm from was not simple, has never been "simple". It can't just be summed up in a box or a one line statement. It was a question that I had to ask myself and really sit with to discover, "Where do I consider home?" I would get sad, because I realized that I felt as though I really did not have a home.

At times, I felt like my life was fake, that I was the only one who knew of my true existence and experiences. That there was really no one else around to substantiate these things that have occurred in my life because I just had those experiences and I moved on. I had secret soirees and trysts with people that nobody ever knew about. I had a childhood in a house that I no longer live in; that nobody in my family lives in. A neighborhood that I haven't visited in over 30 years.

4

Schools that I attended growing up that I never went back to and revisited.

A family that I was born into that is no longer intact. A family dynamic and structure that changed without my input or a full understanding, but life had to go on. I couldn't really stop the flow of life and ask questions, or sit in the safe place of comfort while my confusion dissipated and a more digestible understanding of reality emerged. I needed time to understand my life and my home base, my existence and my residence and the question, "Where are you from?" was as loaded as a baked potato at Bruno's Barbecue Pit. I do not fucking know. I am from a lot of places. Deal with it.

The reality is this: I was born in Chicago, IL, Cook County hospital, 1974 to my mom who was 20 and my dad, 23. They were married at the time. My mom also had my older sister, from a previous relationship. We were a family: Mom, Dad, my sister, and me. We lived from some time on the South side of Chicago. I do not have much recollection of the happenings of Chicago living. I just know I was born there in 1974. I have a picture of me having a lot of fun with cousins in a mini pool on my grandparents back porch of their house on 1256 E 95th Place, South side of Chicago. I remember more of our visits back to Chicago after moving away than I do of being an actual Chicago resident.

The next place I remember living is in a trailer in Alabama, Redstone Arsenal. I would have to ask questions because the only thing I remember about this place is my mom chasing my sister around the trailer because my sister popped me in the head while my mom was trying to do my hair. And my mom had had enough. Hair braiding, combing, straightening, washing, rolling, perming in some fashion are staples of my life, of Black life in general. Maybe because it is such an involved process that you decided to settle in and just make an event of it.

Oftentimes friends and family would gather around just to have full hair combing, styling sessions or simply make the most of the time together. Sometimes it was rare to be in the presence of someone who can actually, "Do hair" so we have to seize the moment. It was not uncommon to have a long line of, "Hey I'm after

_____ [insert cousin's name of choice]" to make sure you

got a fly hairstyle, too, during any gathering at any time at a family

member's house.

With my family being the one that moved away, those

moments were rare jewels when we got them, but my mom had the

magic hands. She could wash hair, press hair, roll hair, braid hair—

whatever we needed, she could do it. She always kept us well put

together from head to toe, a gift passed down to her from her mother.

Empathy may not be a strong suite, but you better believe you will be

supported, and you will look damn good! Sister's game of pop the

little sister in the head did not sit well with my mom. My sister got a

clear whooping that day, and my hair was very well put together.

Stuttgart, Germany comes up next on the radar. From my

recollection, I lived in Stuttgart from ages 4-8. That had to have been

1978-1982. I have fond memories of living in Germany. We took quite

a few trips: The Eagles Nest, Hitler's Castle. Berchtesgaden Gardens, a

German amusement park. We had friends there and connected with

family that were stationed at Hans Airforce Base, not too far off. We

had the luxury of growing up with our extended family while living

abroad.

Those were indeed precious moments. I developed a real fear of anacondas thanks to one cousin, learned the ways of private eye—first rate detecting thanks to another cousin and his nifty recorder—and took on the adored nick name of Repeat Smith, compliments of my other beloved cousins. My Auntie made delicious cobbler and pie (so I recall, but my Cousin Deidre said this could not be the case. Or maybe it was homemade bread I remember. The memory is fuzzy. Still, when I think of my Auntie I think of love and pie.

Cousin Deidre came through with the laughs and amazing bright smile. And then another cousin, always beautiful, planted dreams of super model living. My older cousins were busy living their young adult lives, but I would have the pleasure of connecting with them later as an adult. I do have a faint memory of a young child being scolded for singing "When I get this feeling, I want sexual healing..." snapping along as the tunes of Marvin Gaye's hit wafted through the van radio. Maybe it was me singing or maybe my young cousin, not quite sure. But there was singing, correction, and Marvin Gaye. That is still one of my favorite songs. Even though I did not have a strong childhood memory of some of my older cousins living abroad, they remembered me and loved me fiercely. This love and these fond thoughts of me sustained me in a way that I would not understand

until my 30s.

Germany was a special place for me. I also made a wonderful

friend. Our families were connected. We became friends in

Kindergarten only to later reconnect in our 40s: Me having relocated

from Houston to Florida, and she was living and working as a therapist

in Atlanta. But I was not from Germany. I lived there for four years,

but I was not from Germany.

I feel as though I am from Texas. We moved from Germany to

El Paso around 1982; I was in the third grade. I lived in El Paso from

third grade through graduation from high school, from age 8 to age

17. This is where I consider my childhood. I went to elementary,

middle school and high school in El Paso. I got my period here. I fell in

love here. I offered my virginity here. I went through puberty and

drank alcohol for the first time and learned to drive, somewhat. I

graduated from El Paso and it holds many of my childhood memories

and experiences. But my life in El Paso is still a little divided and spread

out. My parents separated when I was 9, within one year of moving

from Germany to El Paso. We moved to El Paso and were living on the military base of Fort Bliss. When my parents' marriage became irreconcilable, mom packed Shelly and me up in the middle of the night, or rather early morning, and we moved to the northeast side in an apartment.

Another new life. New friends. New room. New experiences. New culture. New rules. To keep some level of consistency, mom drove us to dad's military base house and dropped us off in the mornings so we could still attend school throughout the school year. I always recognized and appreciated that wisdom and sacrifice, even though I did not know the full measure of it. I am grateful for that measure of consistency and normalcy that they provided for me. It was still a little weird. I learned early on to keep love and intimacy at a distance. At 46 years old, I am still trying to make sense of and maintain my relationship with my Daddy, with all of my close relationships. This is no one's fault. It is my emotional work. There is peace in just noticing this reality.

After that school year, I would spend the rest of my time in El Paso on the Northeast side, loosely connected to Fort Bliss. We would later join a church on the military base, Chapel 4, so that soothed my soul somewhat. I was able to still stay a little grounded through the church. My Northeast life started in Butterfield Trail apartments, where I lived through 4th and 5th grade, later moving to a house on Kellogg Street during my 6th grade year. I am so proud of how hard my mom worked to make sure we had a solid foundation. We were poor, but I never knew it. My older sister did, though. Maybe it was because my head was too far in the clouds or maybe because my mom and sister did such a great job protecting and shielding me or maybe because I was so good at playing make believe, but I did not feel the sting of poverty. They took incredibly good care of me. Mom and sister took exceptionally good care of me, they always have.

I am sure that it must have broken their hearts when I had my nervous breakdown at 23 because all they ever wanted was for me to be safe, to be ok. And that Spring of 1997 was a reality check that I was not ok. I was in danger. I was hurt and broken, and they could not fix me. And I know that broke their hearts. But I was ok even if I was not ok. I was safe and it was not their fault. I grew up in El Paso and had a wonderful childhood. I lived in El Paso from 1982-1992, an amazing decade. I feel like I am from El Paso. El Paso is chorizo and eggs. Dancing the cumbia. Cholos and cholas. "Hey baby que paso...I thought I was your only vato." It is listening to the blaring tunes on the radio of, "I don't want to go to work...just let me lay here. I don't want to go to work, just lay all day here. I don't want to go to work, just play all day here. Oh God I don't want to get up and go to work." It is attending Collins Elementary School and having obstacle course races, drawing diagrams of my mom's smoker's lungs to convince her to stop smoking, a project given by my 6th grade science teacher. It is drawing a blueprint of my house, another assignment. An assignment that showed me I have some hidden skills and I can literally do anything I set my mind to. It is where I crushed on neighborhood boys. Where I learned what it meant to be a Black girl in a world that does not always appreciate the essence of Black Girl Magic or the way Black girls show up.

It is where I learned colorism before I knew that colorism was a thing. It is where I learned that I would be desired but not always chosen, so I must always choose myself. It is also where I learned to hide in my own skin. Where I learned to look in the mirror and see someone else because my own image was not good enough. My image was too Black or too brown too ethnic or too African...and during those days nobody, including me, wanted to be associated with anything or anyone African. It is where I learned and believed the lies

of colonialism, gentrification, micro-aggressions, and collected buckets

of white tears to try to wash away my blackness. But I love Ole El Paso,

and I would not change a thing. The third language I learned, was

Spanish. The first was English. The second was German. I regret

nothing. All things work together for the good. And God does all things

well.

3

THE HILL: MY MECCA

The identity confusion was not lost on me because what El Paso took away, baby Prairie View A&M University in Prairie View, Texas gave back 10,000-fold. I graduated from Andress High School in 1992. My mom had remarried in 1991. I was glad. I did not want to leave mom there alone. My sister was living in north Texas. I would be alone for the first time in my life. Dad had remarried, living in California. Mom could not come with me to settle me into college because she had to work. I rode the 10 to 12-hour trip to Prairie View with a man I barely knew, my step dad. He was wonderful. But I did not know him. He and my mom had only been married about a year, and I felt like I was living someone else's life. I just followed the script and said my lines when it was my turn to speak. I was dropped off at the dorms. I was now a young adult, but I still felt like a teenager.

I did all the Freshmen orientation things. Got the paperwork cleared. Moved my items into the door room, Suarez-Collins; also known as "The Ghetto". It was by far the worst of the dorms on Prairie View's campus; so bad that it probably should have been condemned.

But it was my new life for at least this year or semester or however long I had to stay here. I did not know the rules. My mind was still in a haze. Mind was still in a fog. Step-Dad and I stayed overnight in Houston with a friend then after getting me moved in, it was time for him to go. "Welp, I guess I'll head out. Good luck," he said firmly. "Love you". My heart dropped. "Leaving?" I squeaked. "As in going away and leaving me...here?" He gave me a hug. Handed me some money. And he made the trek back to El Paso.

After he left I discovered that my dorm had community showers that required shower shoes in addition to shower water temperatures that were either boiling hot or freezing cold. Getting a lukewarm shower was a blessing, as well as getting a shower that had an actual intact shower curtain. Welcome to college life! "

I now lived in a housing project, for the first time in my life. I had a Muslim roommate who liked tuna fish and only used Nation of Islam products. She was from Dallas. She had big hair and a beautiful smile, but I was annoyed because this was unfamiliar and uncomfortable territory. I was on the Hill. My roommate was a stranger. I was dropped off by a stranger, but the stranger that left me was more comforting than the other strangers that I knew even less. I wanted Him to come back. To take me back home. I wanted my mom there, to help make my dorm room beautiful. But my mom was not there. She was at work. He was there. No one that knew me or loved me the way I was familiar with was there. I had my new Muslim roommate with her tuna fish and her big hair and her big smile and her Nation of Islam body products and her South Dallas twang, and we set out to explore our new residence. I was away at college.

I cried for a week. Nobody knew but I was miserable. I learned to wear a mask at Prairie View; a mask that says "I'm okay," even if I am not. But for all the comfort I left in El Paso, Prairie View made up for it with culture, heritage, pride, and beautiful melanin. Even though I felt as though I had lost myself, Prairie View helped me to tap into a well of Black excellence that I never even knew existed. Aside from the obvious fineness served on platters of Alpha Phi Alpha, Kappa Alpha Psi, Omega Psi Phi, Phi Beta Sigma, there were debonaire brothers of Kappa Kappa Psi band fraternity, Rho Chi Psi service organization, The Romeos, and let's not forget our beloved Panther Club brothers. If that wasn't enough, there were the various intellectual powerhouses mixed in with the fine in Engineering, Computer Science, Architecture,

Education, Nursing, Agriculture...You name it [cue Shirley Caesar].

Everything you could ever dream or imagine was on The Hill. I fell in

with the Christian crowd. My nature wanted to run at warp speed into

the boys' dorms, but my conscience told me I would be safe in the

Christian crowd. I only had one intimate relationship, and that was not

until my senior year in high school. I was still very naïve and

inexperienced and searching. I figured there was safety in churchiness,

so I clung closely to all things churchy at Prairie View.

I did join the University choir, which I loved. But I mistakenly

thought the University choir was the gospel choir. I soon found out

during an Alumni dining hall recruitment that the Baptist Student

Movement (BSM), the gospel choir, and the University choir were

nothing alike. They were in fact the Hatfield and McCoy's of Prairie

View A&M choirs. The Jiggaboos and Wannabees. Target and

Walmart. Montagues and Capulets. Any famous feuding rivals, The

University Choir and BSM were they. It was unheard of that I was a

member of both, and for two years I was pressured to choose: You can

get with this or you can get with that!

I eventually chose the gospel choir. Had I stayed in the University Choir, I probably would have gotten a scholarship and really learned to grow my craft as a singer. Though I was not mature enough to see the value of being in the University choir, I did get a solid foundation in chorus. I was an adept enough soprano to be selected for the East Coast tour. I got an F in choir one semester because I was so apathetic and distracted, that I simply stopped going. I got a lot of Fs. I missed a lot of classes. And even with my Christian, goodie good girl mask, I spent a lot of time in Fuller, Alexander, and Holley Hall.

But out of all the gifts that Prairie View gave me, I don't think any are more precious than that of my best friend, Mel. I met her my first day at Prairie View. I did not think she really liked me much, but I was determined. I saw a jewel in her and I was not going to let her go or let her run me away. I love hard. I loved Mel hard and I always will. I loved her instantly and still do today, after over 20 years later.

I stayed at Prairie View from summer of 1992 to Fall of 1997. Prairie View is what connects me to Houston, even though it is 45 miles Northwest of Houston. Prairie View then Houston, after graduation, is what gave me my Southeast Texas roots. Between

Prairie View and Houston, I was introduced to flying roaches, "Ya heard me", chopped and screw music, zydeco, mix tapes, gospel explosion, Yolanda Adams, Kathy Taylor, Kirk Franklin, Classics, Battle of the Bands, Mystikal, and boudin.

4
TEACHER CHRONICLES

It was my very first year teaching. I was only a few years older than the students. My school was considered rough. The district was a known poor district in a neighborhood whose resources were steadily dwindling. Like many African American areas, at one time it had been the hub of the community. Businesses were plentiful, the students were stellar in academics and athletics, and the community was bustling with pride. After years of defunding and underfunding, mixed with unscrupulous financial transactions and fiscal mismanagement, school resources began to dwindle. Businesses in the community began to fail and close down and the community started to die a slow, arduous death. During my three-year stint, the school enrollment had drastically decreased but the community was still holding on, attempting to tread the economic waters. I knew none of this accepting the job. All I knew was that I had gone the whole summer looking for work unsuccessfully.

It was June and this was the last teacher job fair before the school year was to begin. It was my only hope. My parents had given me a lump sum of $3000 that was supposed to see me through the summer. I had a college degree, but no income coming in and a $1500

car with no working AC in the sweltering summertime Houston heat. I

literally drove around town with a gulp-sized pitcher of ice water and a

towel, plus an extra shirt to change into so I could remain cool and

avoid looking like a sweaty mess when I showed up to a job interview.

I walked into the gymnasium with a mixture of hope, dread, and

despair, trying desperately not to look pathetic. My allowance was

dwindling down to almost nothing. I needed *somebody* to offer me a

job...today. I could not leave that job fair without being hired, and at a

decent salary. It did not matter that I had absolutely no idea about

what I was doing; or of what was in store. I needed a job, TODAY!

My outfit of choice: Power red blazer with black accent

buttons and pocket flaps with a pair of black slacks. My hair tightly

pulled back into a high bun. I channeled my best version of Miss

Westlake from the Cosby show: Theo's stoic yet alluring English

teacher. I stood a mere 5 foot even, weighing slightly over 120

pounds. But I needed a job. Because I had decided the summer before

my senior year in college that I no longer desired to be a child

psychologist, I needed a back-up plan. My major in psychology would

not afford me the opportunity to earn income right out of college. I would have to get my Master's then my PhD before I could make any decent money; and I was already broke. I could not imagine more of the same after graduation. A broke college student is an acceptable cliché. Everyone expects college students to be broke and hungry with a sack full of dirty clothes. But I could not fathom being a broke adult after college. I needed to make a decent living. For me, at the time, a decent living was a salary as close to $30K as I could get. That is only because I overheard someone mention 36K being a really good salary. I had no clue about how much my life cost. This was in 1997. My college crush got an offer to work at a chemical plant making close to $40K. I still had no clue what I was going to do. Walking from a psychology class one day, I saw a sign for the teacher Alternative Certification Program (ACP). It was a program that allowed non-education majors to take classes towards earning an education degree if they declared a major or a minor in a subject that offered a teaching certification. I had always enjoyed children, had literally been around them most of my adolescent life. If I was not entertaining someone's child, I was baby-sitting them or teaching them how to do something, so I suppose teaching had always been a part of me. I did not choose teaching, teaching chose me.

I remember sitting in the teacher's lounge years later as an adult hearing another teacher talk about the "apartment kids". They talked about them like they were some kind of epidemic that was permeating throughout the atmosphere; like some foreign substance that had polluted the drinking water. They were talking about me. I was an apartment kid. My mother, my sister and I lived in an apartment for many years after my parents divorced. They were talking about ME, my situation. I was that statistic! But I was a teacher. A credentialed professional. I graduated high school. I went to college. I earned my master's degree. I got my PhD. But I was still an apartment kid. To them. I was still an apartment kid. I learned that day that there was a stigma attached to living in an apartment. I had never before even imagined that there was anything wrong with apartment living.

The two teachers were huddled at the coffee maker, their jovial chatter wafting through the teacher's lounge. It was a sunny day, and being a teacher new to the district, I had not yet made many friends. Plus, it was the issue of my blackness, or at least that's how I felt, that provided an opening for white teachers to ask me bizarre questions about how to teach Black children. I was the only Black teacher in an English department with fifteen other teachers, and I wore it as both an apology and a badge of honor. I felt pride in being astute enough to be the sole Black teacher among the other white faculty, and I also felt like I was the representation for the whole Black educator existence. As if any err on my part was a permanent scourge upon the scroll of blackness. I felt the weight of Black excellence on my shoulders. So, when I heard them trading stories at the expense of the Black children on the campus, I was torn. How could I be teacher and be Black at the same time without offending or betraying one membership for the sake of the other? It was both the blessing and the curse of double consciousness.

Then there was the time my white teacher co-worker asked me, with all the sincerity in her voice and curiosity in her heart, "Tamia, how do you teach the African American kids to stop using the "be" verb incorrectly?" I looked at her puzzled. She stared back quizzically, patiently waiting for me to respond. "The same way you would teach anyone else," was the only reply I could muster at the time. Like really? How could that even be a legitimate question? But in her world of whiteness and white privilege she never had to consider the lives of people of color, their culture, their ways, their talents, especially as they related to her own. Her safe haven of whiteness was devoid of the Black experience until she became the white teacher of a classroom of Black children, and suddenly their blackness became her impediment. She was forced to consider it. Forced to see it. And she saw it as a problem.

To this day I am embarrassed at my response. I should have had a better, snappier comment. I should have been able to make her realize the discrimination that she was showing. The bias. The micro-aggressions. The hegemony. The division she was perpetuating. I should have been able to teach her to form better and more authentic relationships with her students. I should have known more myself about how to teach conjugation. Hell, I was struggling my damn self with teaching anybody, let alone "African American" kids how to correctly conjugate. But I didn't have a better response. And I often wonder if I missed an opportunity. If I let a teachable moment slip through my fingers to teach my fellow coworker about her privilege and the value that those African American kids brought with them to class. I will never know. But I do know that I was those kids. I was more like those kids than I wanted to admit at times. I thought that to teach them I had to be separate. I had to show them that I knew more.

That I was more refined. That I was polished and well read. I did not want to set a poor example. So, I was plastic instead. A fake, empty vessel.

That's when LaTasha called me out.

"Why you so ghetto?" her words darted and landed at my feet like a luggie, as she looked me up and down. Feeling cheap and well, ghetto, I opened my mouth to speak, but only a flippant scoff came out "Hmph" I smirked, "Excuse me?" In classic defense mode, I doubled down on the authoritarianism. I am the teacher. And I will assert myself, even if just to save face. Poor move on my part, and LaTasha knew it. She was not letting up. I had nowhere to escape to. Twenty-five pairs of eyes stared back at me, awaiting my response. I had just snapped using the most common "hood response" I knew "Y'all got me bent!". It did not fare well for me. It backfired quicker than an abandoned civil war musket. LaTasha, delivered her scathing dissent with such clarity and eloquence with a scowl to match. I knew that I was out of my element. Though I saved face that day, I also made a commitment to be better and do better as a Black woman and a Black teacher. That was the issue. I had no clue how to be any of those:

Black. Woman. Teacher. My own perception of what that meant was

still developing and here I was tasked with being responsible for

leading others. I did not know how to fit the me that I was familiar

with into that space and still be comfortable. Like always, I role played.

I had a long way to go.

5

Flashback: Supercuts

I could usually feel the person staring at me from across the room. Then a few minutes later I would hear, "Can I touch your locs?" I would usually oblige them and say yes, even though having someone touch my hair is just as personal as someone coming up to me and saying, "Do you mind if I rub your butt?" It's my personal space, but since people are so intrigued by it, I allow them to share in my experience. It's my way of sharing myself with them, my way of helping them to understand me. I wasn't always this proud of my hair or my heritage. At one point, I did everything I could to keep from being identified as the stereotypical Black girl. It wasn't that I didn't want to be Black. It was just that being anything but Black seemed to be so much better. Other races didn't have the nappy hair or the wide noses and big lips. Those features were looked upon as being ugly, and I didn't want to be ugly. If being Black meant being ugly, I didn't want any part of it.

I first saw Diana Ramirez's haircut in my 7th grade Social Studies class. She walked in and it was perfect. Everyone flocked around her, oohing and awing her new style. "It's layers," she said excitedly, "I got it done at Supercuts". "Supercuts?" I thought. I could afford that. They had a $7 special, and I knew I had the money. That week, I convinced my mother to take me there. I know that she knew my Supercuts obsession was the wrong direction to go in, but this was a lesson I needed to learn and feel. She let me pay for the $7 Diana Ramirez special at Supercuts. I sat in the chair with hopeful anticipation of how my new layers would look. I imagined how the whole class would flock around me too and ooh and awe, and gawk over my makeover. I would outshine Diana's hair. My Supercut's style would be the newest topic of interest. It would be an interesting topic, indeed. Just not the one that I was hoping for. When the stylist whirled me around, my face fell flat. It was horrible. It looked nothing like Diana Ramirez's hair. I was mortified.

My hair. My little Black girl hair. My kinky, coily tresses; the ones that grow up to meet the Sun, these tresses were chemically straightened. They were chopped and cut in jagged edges, lying flat to my head, and tucked awkwardly behind my ears, only the chopped tresses couldn't reach fully behind my ears, so they kept popping out. It was a side ear cowlick that would not stay down. My Black girl hair was not made to be cut in layers for $7 at Supercuts. I was

inconsolable.

The next day, I locked myself in the bathroom before

school and refused to come out. I couldn't let anyone see me like this

with these short, butchered pieces all over my head. I looked like a

scalped chicken; like a cock fighting rooster way past the prime of

victory. "I'm not coming out!" I screamed agony at my sister who tried

to lovingly cajole me out of the bathroom. When that didn't work, her

soft words falling short, she brought in the enforcer. I lost the battle

when my sister called my mother at work, and my mother then

demanded that I leave the bathroom and go to school. No more

discussion. I could visualize how tightly my mom was holding her lips

by how each word squeaked out through the phone:

Get. Your. Ass. Out. Of. That. Damn. Bathroom. And. Go. To.

School.

But mom, I whimpered

Tamia take your ass to school. Now!

My sister gathered what she could of my chopped hair, pulled it back into a puny little pig tail, and sent me off to school. For good measure, she tied a pink bow around it. The bow obviously overshadowing the actual hair. I was greasy. I was sad. I was mortified. I was on my way to school. Shit!

To my surprise, when I got to school, my friends didn't embarrass me like I thought they would, but they convinced me to take my hair down, remove the pig tail and just wear it free. They said it didn't look that bad, but I knew different. It wasn't like Diana Ramirez's hair.

I wish I could say that I learned to embrace who I was that day, but it would take at least 28 more years for that lesson to take root. Society didn't make being a Black girl easy, especially if you weren't a Black girl with long wavy hair and light skin. I had to grow into who I was as an African American woman and completely embrace everything about myself.

So that's why I did it. That's why I cut my hair. I had to see what was underneath all of those chemicals and get to the root of who I was.

I stood in the mirror and stared at the spongy mass that was on the top of my head. I looked at it curiously wondering what lie beneath all that perm. Why did I try so hard to disguise my true hair texture? What was so ugly about it? I did what every Black woman dreads: the big chop. I cut it off. I cut off all the perm and chemicals that I had been using to hide my "ugliness" for years. As each piece fell, glimpses of my true self began to emerge. I was not only cutting away my permed hair. I was cutting away society's perceptions of me, of who I was as a woman. As a Black woman. I cut away the shame and embarrassment of everything that comes with being Black and woman. I was freeing myself from other people's opinions. This time, I didn't expect to see Diana Ramirez when I turned around and looked in the mirror. I expected to see me. Whoever me was. I was ready to meet her.

This was the first time I went natural. That sounds so funny saying it, "Went natural". You would think that we would say, "I returned to my natural state or reverted", something indicating that we were simply letting our natural essence come forth. It would be a long journey, my reverting back to my natural hair. I can truly say that it is a journey I am still on. I discovered that returning to the natural state of my hair had levels to it. It has levels that I am not even certain

I have reached yet. Actually, I am definitely certain I have not reached

all of the levels of this naturalness. The first time I "reverted". I had

this baby afro and absolutely no direction about what to do with my

hair. I didn't know anything about textures, curl pattern 4C, Z curl, S

Curl, blah...blah...blah. This was before the newest Natural girl, Curly

girl movement, the expansion of YouTube videos, Style Blogs, and

#BlackGirlMagic that we have now. There were no support groups or

healing circles, helpful tips or shelves full of products to support my

journey. Those who knew what to do, and had the secret sauce of

successful transitioning, were not spreading that wealth. Those of us

who were interested in crossing over, we had to venture out on our

own and learn the hard way.

It was around 2001 and I just had an itching in my soul to cut

my perm off. The weather had been extremely unpredictable in

Houston, and my mind went quickly back to how my life revolved

around what my hair could or could not handle: moisture, rain,

humidity, pool water. It just all seemed so limiting, and for what? I was

permed, or relaxed. My hair was chemically straightened and had

been for at least twenty years or so. My new curiosity was sparked by a picture I saw of Bertrice Berry, the author and motivational speaker. I had read one of her books, and turned it over to the back, seeing her profile picture. She looked so regal. So authoritative. I knew then that I wanted to be a writer and I just thought that writing, professors and locs went hand in hand. My first determinant for getting locs was to simply look academic and author-like. It was purely cosmetic. I liked how locs looked. It had nothing to doing with Rastafarianism or #blackgirlmagic, #blacklivesmatter, or any other movement other than the fact that I wanted people to take my scholarship and my writing seriously and I was convinced that locs were the way to go. Yes, I was just that shallow. A little later into the journey, I did begin to think a little deeper. I thought about how I really felt about me. About my hair. My features. And I wanted to be able to accept myself completely without pretense. Something I am still trying to be: Authentic.

This deeper level of acceptance, though, I am convinced is a life journey and not a destination. I believe that, somehow, I am always going to discover new parts of myself and be nudged to accept yet another self or aspect of myself that is revealed. I always seem to be presented with a new challenge to like or accept myself or reject myself. If it wasn't my hair, it was my small frame. If not my small frame, it was my intellect. If not my intellect, it was my prestige. If not

my prestige, it was my network. If not my network, then my drastic

mood swings. If not the mood swings, then the moments of

listlessness or depression or exuberance or…The list went on and on,

but this time I wanted to like myself completely, and I felt that

reverting to my natural state was the way to do it. What I would later

discover was that in reverting to my natural hair, I opened that door to

acceptance of myself in a myriad of ways that I never knew were

necessary. First, I accepted my baby afro. It was a pitiful little afro. It

had no form or shape. The texture was brittle and jagged. But the

compliments poured in, "Oh look at your eyes, they are so beautiful.

I've never really seen them before. Your short hair brings out your

beautiful eyes," one of my white co-workers complimented. Then I

learned from my roommate, a sister, that I needed to edge and taper

my little afro. It was not as on point as I thought. But yet, I still felt

beautiful. I was beginning to see beauty in myself in places I had never

seen before.

Comparison and judgement set in. Even with the embracing of

my natural state, I was trying to be an acceptable Naturalista: What

should my hair look like? I faced the dilemma of what to do with natural hair in Houston's humid weather. As it grew, I became more aware of my hair and its texture. I tried so many different products. It was greasy. It was dry. It was brittle. It was dripping wet. I looked like an extra on Coming to America, auditioning for the Soul Glo couch scene. And I was clueless. I just didn't know what to do with it. It was there and big and untamed. I didn't have enough for an afro puff, and I dreaded using a head band for fear that I would look like one of the babies with the thin head band who barely had enough hair to accent with a band. I didn't know why having short hair was taboo. I think in regards to religious doctrine, the Black community took the scripture, "A woman's crown is her glory" to another oppressive level; a level that was never the intent of the scripture. We used it to criticize and loathe ourselves and each other, to separate and re-oppress, pass judgement and self-hate. I just didn't want to be the object of derision. I was a high school teacher, always under strict scrutiny, a microscope. I just did not want that negative attention. I experimented. I played with it. I played with color and twisting and weave and all those fun accessories available to us Black girls and our hair. One day, early in my career, out of a fit of rage, one of my students called me a "bald headed bitch". I still don't know what I was more offended by: being called bald headed, or being called a bitch. I

responded the way any novice teacher with an ounce of hood would,

"Your mama's a bald-headed bitch!" Don't worry, I got better. I was

called bitches much more during my career, but I promise my

responses evolved. As I grew and learned, and became more secure in

who I was, I not only was called a bitch less and less, but if or when I

was called one, I had a better response. Oftentimes the response was

gentler, recognizing that aggression as trauma provoked that needed a

trauma informed response. Later, I learned to not respond in words

but to respond with space. Space for love. Space for healing. Space for

correction. Space for forgiveness. Space for acceptance. But those

encounters are for a different chapter, perhaps even a different book

PART TWO

DISCOVERY

6

MANIA

I sat on the cold, dark pavement of the church parking lot rocking back

and forth and glaring up into the starry sky. I'm safe here.

Seven…seven…seven…the "number of perfection." The good number,

I muttered to myself unintelligibly. The parking lot was littered with

painted numbers that glowed under the morning light. My eyes stayed

fixed upon the number seven. Seven made me feel safe, so I sat there

as though clinging to life itself. "As long as I stay on 7, I'm safe." I

babbled inwardly, going in and out of consciousness. Six was bad. Six

made me feel anxious. I had always learned that six was bad. I could

not sit on six or even look at the number six. Seven was my safe place.

And there I sat. Off in the distance, the stolen car door was still ajar

and engine running. It roared at me, so I had to get out. It wasn't safe.

It was evil. Only evil cars roar. I had to get to a safe place. Blue is safe.

Seven is safe. Light is safe. Church is safe.

I didn't intend to take her car. I just wanted to be safe. I thought the

car was mine; that God had brought it back to me because he knew I

needed it. He knew I was hurting, that I needed a way to get to work.

That I was going to lose my job because I had no way to work. My engine was blown. Mr. Blount said he could fix it. It's been almost a year with him having my car. He no longer answers his phone. It's disconnected. He let me use his car while mine was in the shop being fixed. But then one day I came outside, and it was just gone. I called Mr. Blount and he said, his wife needed it back. Today at work, this car looked just like mine, the one Mr. Blount let me use. The one that disappeared. I saw her drive up in it, so I knew that it had come back to me. I asked for her keys, to get something from the car. I drove off in it. But she said it was not my car, it was her car. But it looked like mine. Mr. Blount said I could drive it. He said it was mine for as long as I needed it while he fixed my car. But then it was gone. I came outside to go to work, and it was gone. I needed to go to work. How was I going to get there? I did not have any more "sick days." The school was going to dock my pay. I was going to lose my job. I wasn't going to be able to survive or support myself. My parents didn't have any more money to give me. No one knows me. I live alone. I needed my car. Where's my car?

The church said pray. I prayed. The church said fast. I fasted. The church said believe. I believed. But I was sad. I couldn't sleep. I listened for God. I heard him. He said go. He said take the car. He said

sacrifice for me. Don't eat. Keep your temple clean. So, I didn't eat. For

one week. I didn't eat. I took a few bites, but not full meals. God had

strengthened me. He was consecrating me. I didn't sleep. I needed to

pray. The church said when you can't sleep at night that God is trying

to tell you something. So, when I went to bed at 11:00pm and woke

up at 1:30am I knew God needed to speak to me. That I needed to

pray for somebody. Somebody needed my prayers. Two-thirty in the

morning. Still praying. I tried to lay down. I tried to sleep. But I wasn't

tired. I needed to clean. God doesn't bless mess. So, when I could not

sleep, and I was done praying, I cleaned. Four-thirty in the morning. It

was time for work. I felt refreshed, like I could parasail to work all on

my own steam. I was bursting with energy. I was so happy, ecstatic. I

don't know why. "This must be what being in God's will feels like," I

thought to myself. I felt like I could do anything. Like I could be

anything. Wisdom, beauty and strength were all mine. They were

endowed to me by the Holy Spirit, so I thought. God had heard my

prayers. He had given me beauty for my ashes. He had given me

strength for fear and gladness for mourning. Yes! My sorrow was over.

Now was my "just reward." Joy abundantly. Peace abundantly. I dressed how I felt, radiantly. I slipped my black crop sweater over my head, stepped into my leopard print tee length form fitting skirt. I put on a pair of sheer black nylons and stepped into my black patent leather shoes. I unwrapped my hair, which fell perfectly in a bob that contoured to my face. No time to eat. I didn't need food. I felt amazing. I was on a high. It felt so good. I don't need food anymore. Wow...this must be how the supermodels stay so thin! They survive off of God's power like me. Oh my God! I'm a supermodel! My uncle told me I would be. He told me my senior pictures looked like I was a model. God did it! Finally! Wait until everybody sees the new me. No more lame Tamia. This is my time!

This was 23-year-old me. The first-year teacher. She was on the cusp of a major, very public nervous breakdown, only she did not know it. She was in phase two of psychosis. But she did not know it. She thought she was doing God's work. That she was being used. She was both right and wrong.

At this time, I must have been taking public transportation. The engine in my car blew out two months after I purchased it, in the heat of summer. Two weeks before school started. I didn't live on a bus line in the North suburbs of Houston—Spring, TX. It was as far north as you could go and still somewhat be in Harris County, yet outside of the Houston City limits. It felt like I was worlds away from everything. I was newly adulting. I was the youngest of two girls, my sister being one who was wholly self-sufficient and protective, and I being one who nestled tightly into her overbearing, protective nature like the cocoon of safety that it was. I had no real urgency to find my own way until I had no choice but to find my own way because all other roads were closed. This was that time. Out from the ark of safety of my sister, Shelly, and my mom, I was vulnerable to the perils of society. The treachery that comes with mixing with the general population who, although they do not directly have an agenda to destroy you, do not feel inclined to protect you either because they assume that you have sense enough to protect yourself or it just simply is not their business. But I was a sponge—a naïve, gullible, optimistic sponge—that soaked up all the world had to offer, whether good or bad. My glasses were far beyond rose colored, they reeked of roses, tulips, azalea, lilies, daffodils and daisies.

Mind as Well

To borrow from a few words of Miss Sophia from The Color Purple, "A girl child" like me with her head in the clouds was not safe in a world full of sinister behavior that was more common than not. I was the outsider. Everything else was the norm. My reality was fantasy come to life; for I wore my heart and every emotion plastered to my forehead and I did not readily separate fact from fiction. I felt so strongly and believed so profoundly that I did not always decipher between dreams, visions, and the present moment. It all swirled together in my mind like a savory gumbo and I could rarely make heads or tails of things. I was losing my mind.

I remember small instances of losing touch with reality. In the 8th grade during a basketball or volleyball practice, I recall sitting on the gym floor being surrounded by my teammates, the loudness of middle school activity swirling around me, and I had an open eyed black out. I didn't pass out or fall out on the floor. I simply became overcome with anxiety because I forgot where I was. My eyes were wide open, I could hear activity all around me, but I was confused, disoriented. From sheer instinct, I breathed in deeply, closed my eyes and began to self-check the things I knew for sure: My name is Tamia. I am in a gym. This is a gym floor (I touched it with my fingers spread wide). I am a Terrace Hills Trojan. I live on Kellogg street. Then I

exhaled: I am safe. I never told anyone about that encounter. I didn't

even realize that it was enough of an encounter to talk about. I did

feel an overwhelming sense of shame and began to develop the

limiting belief that I just might be crazy.

It was my sophomore year of college. I was singing in the

gospel choir. I had always sung. Singing was in my blood. In true gospel

choir fashion, the front row of the choir is the Holy Grail. No one will

ever be on the front row who is not expressive, exuberant,

entertaining, and showy: that is just the gospel choir way. I had made

it to the front row and was holding it down, or so I thought. On this

day, I felt my energy suddenly change. An overwhelming sense of

sadness and listlessness came over me. It seemed as though my

emotions were going haywire. A dullness infiltrated my being, glazing

over my pupils. My light had dimmed. I had not been feeling my best,

emotionally. I was not sure what was going on with me, but I just

could not get out of my own head headspace, things seemed to be

going at warp speed, and I really just wanted to take a nap. Skipping

choir rehearsal was not an option, especially since we were practicing

for the Baptist Student Union (BSU) gospel competition. The weekly choir rehearsals, well into the night...the anxiety of the upcoming

gospel competition...the stress of school and class (of which I was

failing with a 1.9 GPA) ...everything was coming to a head and it was

"written all over my face" because in one motion, our choir director,

Adrian, pointed to me and moved me from the front row to the

second row. It was like he had pierced my soul. I complied. But I

suppose it took a minute for the emotions to bubble to the top

because a few moments after my demotion, the tears came streaming

down and an uncontrollable wail burst through my lips. I could not

stop wailing. It was an audible cry. I was either 19 or 20. Here I was

wailing like an insolent child. I was bleeding out emotionally and

hurting everywhere. I ran to a door to try to leave, but it was locked,

which added to the embarrassment and anxiety and wailing. My

friends came to me to usher me away and help me out through an

unlocked exit door, but the damage had been done. Now everyone

knew that I was not ok. My mask was shattered, my cover was blown.

I just might be crazy. And now other people know, as well.

Exuberant emotions were always a part of who I was. My

parents often joked that I would play until I dropped, and wherever I

dropped is where I would stay and sleep. I would actually sleep wherever I dropped down. We love to tell a story of the ringing door

bell and sleeping Tamia. I had to have been about 6 or 7 years old. We

were stationed in Germany at the time; my dad was an active-duty

army enlisted soldier. I had lost my two front teeth, of which I was

ecstatic because now I could legitimately sing the Sesame Street tune,

"All I want for Christmas is my two front teeth." I was a hyper child.

The school officials wanted to place me on Ritalin, but my mom

declined, opting to simply keep me actively involved in as many sports

as were available: Soccer, T-ball, Ballet, gymnastics, cheerleading,

Brownies...I was always doing something physical and constructive (as

the older generation loves to suggest). My mind was constantly

occupied. On this day, we were at home: Mom, dad, Shelly and I—the

doorbell rang. In my hyper, hoppy self, I exclaimed, "I'll get it!" In true

overactive fashion, I dashed towards that ringing doorbell, bouncing

all along the way. Minutes later the doorbell was still ringing. My

family were all confused, "I thought Tammy went to get the door?"

They looked around at each other, puzzled. My dad went to

investigate, and there he found me: inches from the door, snuggled on

the floor, sleep. One hand outstretched, as though still trying to

complete the task of opening the door, the other with two fingers in my mouth (I sucked my two fingers well beyond an acceptable age).

He burst into full laughter.

That story is shared to show both my excitable nature and my

need for slumber. And of course, to show how I will sleep anywhere at

any time if my body is ready to turn off. We often compare me to the

energizer bunny, both then and now. When I'm on, I'm on, happily

rolling along energetically beating my drum of choice. But when I'm

off, I'm off. And, just like the dying battery-operated bunny, I slow to a

warped stall. Wherever I am, in which ever task I am engaged, I slowly

wind down to a total halt, find a spot to sleep and sleep. My life has

become a balancing act between being off and on, doing what I need

to do to be more on than off, but also honoring my off time and self

and in fact, making room to be off. I now realize that my nature is

neither to operate constantly at warp speed, at sloth state, or airy

cloud, but I am all of these things. Letting go of the stigma that comes

with having a mental health condition is a major part of my journey of

growth and change. It has taken me twenty years to arrive at this

place of emotional freedom, and yet, the journey continues.

Mind as Well

7
PHASES

The first phase of my journey, I dealt with the reality of taking medication. I was an avid Christian who believed wholeheartedly in divine, supernatural healing: baptismal by fire, speaking in tongues, and the laying on of hands. I learned that in college. I grew up in non-denominational, Baptist, and Methodist settings. I continued attending a charismatic church after I graduated from college, and I was extremely active, but they did not know much about me. They did not know that I was on the verge of a break down.

A consequence of mental health conditions is the intermittent relationships and difficulty maintaining consistent, close ties, even with family members at times. When my breakdown occurred, no one in my immediate social circle really knew me. They knew that I was talented and social, but not much else. The blessing of the church is that in my crises, they did rally around to protect me. To the average person passing by, I could have be any crazy vagrant. They did not know that I came from a loving family, was a Prairie View A&M University graduate, a beloved teacher, sister and daughter. They did not know that I was not a threat to anyone or myself. That I was only frightened, desperately in need of rest, love and nourishment. I was found wandering the streets of northeast Houston, begging for people to help me. I managed to call a few church members, whose numbers I could recall, telling them that I was afraid and did not know what was happening to me. This is how they were able to find me and send help. Even in this completely unraveled state, I was protected, and am still truly grateful. This was 1998. It was my first-year teaching, and it was also when I hit rock bottom.

During the next phase of my journey, I dealt with working to become an advocate for myself in learning more about my condition, setting boundaries, and taking medication; learning coping skills, setting routines and developing de-escalation strategies and speaking up for myself with medical professionals to adjust the medication. Oftentimes the medication that I took had adverse affects. One medication had me gain close to 70lbs, and another placed me in a nearly catatonic state where I could only stand, stare, drool and mumble. This catatonic state occurred during back-to-school preparation week while I was trying to decorate my classroom to teach the new batch of students for the oncoming year.

I stood at the chalkboard staring for at least two hours. I was trying to write my name on the board. Unpacked boxes of bulletin board boarder, stenciled letters, and grammar and writing posters set in a mound in the center of the classroom. School was set to begin in exactly 7 days, and I could not even form a coherent sentence.

"Tamia?" My department chairperson called out after passing my room for the third time. She entered the doorway only and looked at me. We had talked previously about my mania and depression. She shared some of her own journey. But our lives were different. She was a white woman. I was a Black woman. No one in my family, in my circle, spoke so freely about mental health conditions unless we were calling someone else "crazy", talking about getting a Social Security Check, or telling someone to "go get checked" because they were being irrational. My circle did not talk freely about navigating the mental health system, especially in relation to ourselves. Society did not make room to be Black and unwell, then live to tell that hero's journey.

"Tamia," her voice broke in again from the doorway. "You need to get off of whatever you are on." She noticed? A sigh of wonder and relief rushed over me. I was trying to sprint but could only crawl at a snail's pace. I thought I had to just take whatever

medication I was prescribed. Until she said that, I was not aware of my

agency as a client. I spoke to the psychiatrist about the medication. I

told my psychiatrist that I could not function, and I needed something

else. He and his nurse worked with me to find another medication

after I had been on the snail's pace medication for nearly two months.

I was discovering my voice as an advocate for myself in telling the

doctor that I did not like the way something made me feel, that I

deserved to define quality of life for myself. I would later find out that

tapping into how something made me feel would be important in all

things, especially with nutrition. Within a week of stopping the old

medication and beginning the new one, I started feeling like my old

sane self again. My life had some sense of normalcy again. My energy

level rose, and my clarity of thinking returned. Eventually the extra

weight dropped off, too. I was regaining a sense of balance.

The newest phase of my journey brought me to a place where

I was no longer able to take the medication that had centered me, that

I had adjusted doses of so that my weight could normalize and I would

be able to interact with others. I had created a healthy balance of

psychotherapy, coping mechanisms, medication, and consistency, yet my body was rejecting the medicine. And it is in this phase that I learned the power of what I consider the trifecta: a nutritious diet, stress-managing lifestyle, and healthy movement that intentionally work to keep my body fit and able to release both internal and external toxins.

I learned that many of the symptoms that I had been experiencing nearly all my entire life were the same symptoms of estrogen dominance, the same symptoms that show up when there are toxins in the body, the exact same symptoms that emerge when there is a type of imbalance in the body, the same symptoms that emerge with poor digestion or a diseased gut and the same symptoms of unprocessed emotions. Digestion in this sense relates to the intake of all things: food and other people's emotions. They are all a form of energy that needs a place to go. Being unaware of this can create emotional or energetic build-up or even blockages. In my life, this energy manifested itself as emotional and physical trauma, and disease through psychosis and uterine fibroid tumors. Slowly building up a lifestyle of wellness that supports my whole well-being would take time, intention, and awareness. Each time I felt like I discovered "the Holy Grail" of wellness, I learned about yet another layer.

Even more recently, I learned about inflammation in the brain, which contributes to psychosis and can be directly connected to inflammation in the body. The recommendation by the British Journal of Psychiatry is as I stated above: whole food plant based anti-inflammatory diet, mindfulness through deep breathing, and stress balancing exercise routine such as yoga, Tai Chi or Qigong. I became a certified yoga, meditation, and Qigong instructor and adopted a whole-food, plant-based diet in order to better understand living mindfully. Then I learned that mindfulness is a whole complete field of its own with a framework. I now sit in digital communities supporting one another: Sangha, African studies groups, Yoga philosophy groups, Peer support spaces. I eventually became a facilitator and co-facilitator in these spaces as well. During this phase of my journey, I found yoga and meditation. I found eating for wellness. I found community. I found myself. And in this phase I learned that I had to be willing to forget everything I had ever learned about wellness, health, relationships, community and nutrition and be willing to re-educate myself and be open to what makes sense to me. Get back to basics about my mind and body work; my connection with others; my place in this world. Then I would need to put it all back together again in essentially that same place but with a new understanding. I learned

that I must be intentional about my wellness—my existence. It may

sound archaic or vague or unrealistic. Some may even say my

viewpoint is superficial and unrelatable, but honestly, it is these things

mentioned above, and these lessons learned below that have kept me

alive and well. There is no in between: It's either Life or Death.

Here are a few nuggets of wellness wisdom that I have picked up along

the way:

1. Psychosis, anxiety, chronic depression can be traced to inflammation

    in the brain which can be detected by a simple blood test. The

    recommended treatment for such is anti-inflammatory whole foods, a

    plant-based diet, stress reducing breathing & exercise regimen, and

    movement such as yoga, tai chi or Qigong. It's that simple, but it is not

    easy.

2. Stress in the body releases a hormone called *cortisol*, which releases

    adrenaline and uses our *progesterone* and then releases *glucose* in our

    bodies, which pads us up so we can live. Therefore, stress makes us

    fat. The more fat we have, the more estrogen we have and the less progesterone we have. Progesterone is the hormone needed to keep estrogen from over producing. If our progesterone is used up by protecting us from chronic stress, it cannot keep the estrogen in check. The result is Estrogen Dominance. Be in Peace.

3. Digestion is key to being well. Nutrients are absorbed in our gut. Stress affects how well we absorb nutrients because stress directly affects our intestines. Emotions and our gut (Gastrointestinal Tract) are intimately linked together. The gut is often referred to as "Our Second Brain". Therefore, we can heal our gut by healing our mind and heal our mind by healing our gut. They work together both ways. Our heart contains our other brain. Mind, Heart, Gut: Think Feel, Digest (Absorb). There are many pathways to wellness. Relax.

4. Food as medicine. The right nutrients and minerals can heal our minds and bodies or at least give us enough energy and endorphins to participate in life. We can literally eat ourselves well. Remember that. Nutritional deficiency assessments can help pinpoint our focus of which vitamins or minerals our body most needs.

5. Laughter or Joy as medicine. Dr. Brené Brown says that Joy and gratitude create the pathways for our journey. Wallowing, though it feels good, is the emotional narcotic that keeps us addicted to being

unwell. Does that mean that we "feel" happy all the time? No, of course not. But it does mean that we do *feel* all the time and we see and understand that all things are related. It is a matter of perspective. This takes the mystery out of, "What is wrong with me?" or "Why am I feeling this way?" There are a myriad of reasons, but there are also a few simple solutions that can be implemented and kept in rotation along the way. One is to feel your feelings and release them. We can simply BE without the pressure to DO or even to Understand. Just BE.

6. Gratitude, Accountability, and Acceptance are key to wellness. Holding on to grudges or blaming others for any misfortune I encounter along the way without taking ownership of my part, being gentle and forgiving with myself and others, and accepting both what I do and what I do not have control over, all impact my overall wellness: mentally, emotionally and spiritually. They eventually make an impact socially, occupationally, financially, environmentally and intellectually. Knowing that all these things are interrelated, in that, they provide a gateway or pathway for other parts of me to flourish or create roadblocks to wellness is paramount.

7. Nature is our healer and teacher. Connecting with nature and understanding the natural process of things: body, environment, social

structures, astronomy, astrology, physiology, etc., can help us to better understand others and ourselves. Knowing that there is nothing new under the sun, and that the first time I learned something I most likely only retained a small portion of it, depending on the situation and my state of mind at the time, may help me to remember that I have all I need. Sometimes I need to revisit and (re)learn it with fidelity instead of adopting something entirely new. As with nature, the sun will rise in the east. It will set in the west. The moon will go through its seven phases and the planets will rotate around the sun. Birds will fly south. Leaves will change colors. Tides will rise and flowers will bloom. Petals will fall. For everything there is a season. I have learned that I am happiest when I am in harmony with nature, or at least as close to it as possible. My goal is to slow down or speed up enough to not just survive or coexist, but thrive as I was naturally intended to.

8. Processed sugar can be as addictive (if not more) than cocaine. Wait what? Why then, for the love of all things holy, do we as a society give sugar to infants and children, whose brains do not fully develop until their early 20s? Why? My only guess is that we do it because it's what we know. And it is what we know because it is what we have been marketed and targeted to know. I am certainly not trying to sound like

a conspiracy theorist, but the science behind the damaging and

harmful effects of sugar is real. It is not new, and yet, I was fourty-two

years old when I found out by my own experience. Perhaps it was

taught to me at an early age, but the fact remains: Business as usual

leads to decline in wellness. Intentional wellness requires un-

maintaining the status quo, especially if the status quo is not centered

in equitable or critical well-being.

9. Connecting with others is an essential human trait that is affected by

how well we connect with our own selves. Self-knowledge,

acceptance, love, and patience are essential for connection with

others. Healing and growth starts from within: they are inside jobs.

Even if I flourish outwardly, at some point it has to resonate deeply

within me. This is easier for some than others, but it is essential to us

all as human beings. Love in its truest form is the common

denominator. Love for self = Love for all beings. Ubuntu, the South

African word which means humanness is fully expressed in the South

African proverb *Ubuntu ngumtu ngabanye abantu*, which translates:

"A person is a person through other people". *Ubuntu*, the South

African term meaning *humanness*, is found through our

interdependence, collective engagement, and service to others.

10. "Bodies are made for movement". Being active can heal, just as needed rest. Building regular activity into my routine is a plus for me. It has kept me from popping a pain pill and even brought me out of a depressive or rage spiral. Breath and Movement have given me energy and redirected excess energy as well. Movement can be seen as medicine, as well.

11. Create space. Hold space. Take up space. Share space. Sitting with myself, knowing myself intimately is healing and freeing. I cannot get from outside what I do not activate on the inside. I can observe someone else's peace practice, but I can only sustain when I make it my own. We are guides who introduce each other to our own selves. Our journeys, though interconnected, are ours alone.

12. Breath is life. Regulating, observing, connecting with our breath is life itself. Life begins and ends with breath. The practice of yoga calls it *Pranayama*, a Sanskrit term. Also referred to as Breath work or Deep breathing, tapping into breath regulation is a critical key to wellness.

8
PIECES OF MY MIND

Since the psychotic episode "happened to me" at 23, I spent many years trying to unravel that situation and truly understand both myself and what "happen to me". I wondered if it was an awakening, a belief expansion, a consciousness rising, or sheer insanity.

Sometimes a psychotic break can float into our lives on the wings of our faith, hope, and prayer if our belief systems are not rooted in a way for us to be and stay grounded and make peaceful sense of new or unfamiliar information. That was my story. I believe that since my actual nature is to approach the world with completely open arms, I took a lot of complex biblical or spiritual concepts literally and did not have the lived personal experiences or mental capacity to fully handle the deep and complex information that I came in contact with. In many belief systems, you must have a mentor to study ancient texts and be a certain age to begin your studies. In my case, this mental, emotional, and spiritual overload was exacerbated by poor nutrition, lack of sleep, financial strain, and stressful conflicts at work, in my personal life and with my volunteer organizations. Multiple elements were pulling on my mind all at once, and I did not know it. I did not know it because I did not know how to make peace with and maintain peace in my mind: Boundary setting.

Because I come from a family network where religion and spirituality are a central guiding force, I cannot help but to wonder where faith and belief fit in the spectrum of psychosis, consciousness, mental wellness and recovery. A few models and some personal life experiences have helped me have a clearer picture of how all these factors could be true. It may be simply a matter of perspective and cultural lens. Since I am not a theologian, but theology and faith have been such major factors in framing how I think, thereby crafting who I am, I felt the need to have a more foundational view of theological references to psychosis. Since I also used traditional western pharmaceutical treatment, I feel compelled to spotlight that experience. Since nutrition and health played a major factor, I must shed light on how nutrition, exercise, mindful movement, and yoga have impacted my peace of mind. Since meditation and expanded spirituality such as Buddhist mantra, Hindu principles (Sutras), South African Philosophy (Ubuntu) have brought clarity, I must shed light on how embracing spirituality has brought peace within my mind.

PRAYING METTA: LOVING KINDNESS & COMPASSION

May I be safe from inner and outer harm.

May I be healthy and strong.

May I be happy and content.

May I live with ease of well-being.

May you/she/he/they be safe from inner and outer harm.

May you/she/he/they be healthy and strong.

May you/she/he/they be happy and content.

May you/she/he/they live with ease of well-being.

May we be safe from inner and outer harm.

May we be healthy and strong.

May we be happy and content.

May we live with ease of well-being.

*A Buddhist prayer

9
LIFE IN PEACE & PRACTICE

Since I intend to live in peace, I now see my mind as a whole and complete part of me that can be influenced by a myriad of things. I really protect my peace at all costs: whatsoever things are good. Whatsoever things are loving. Whatsoever things are kind. Whatsoever things are of good rapport. Think on these things. I intend to bring peace to wherever I go. I have found the only way to do this is to stay in peace within my mind, body, and spirit.

Meditation helps, but meditation was really that last stage of my peace process. Meditation in terms of a physical sitting took a while for me to ease into. I meditated on principles of peace and wellness. I accepted myself, my mind included as well in every stage, and gave myself permission to bring peace to parts of me that were disturbed if that was physically, emotionally, or mentally possible, and I learned the power of letting go of all expectations beyond me. Letting go even to the point of letting go of people: I own no one. No one owns me. My

peace is mine.

"IF YOU CONTROL YOUR MIND, YOU HAVE CONTROLLED EVERYTHING.
THEN THERE IS NOTHING IN THIS WORLD TO BIND YOU."

YOGA SUTRA 2 OF PATANJALI

My first full encounter with yoga was in the summer of

2018 during yoga teacher training with <u>Breathe for Change</u> in

Tampa, Florida. Before this 16-Day, 200-hour intensive, I did not

have an established yoga practice. I was not at all familiar with

the 8-Fold Path or 8 Limbs of Yoga. I had no conscious knowledge

of Ayurveda, the nutritional science and Sister practice to yoga. I

was not familiar with yoga's roots of the concept of "Living Yoga

off the mat." I was not even aware of the asanas, their Sanskrit

pronunciation or even that the written language was Sanskrit.

I came to yoga looking for a place to put my emotions.

Though I was not conscious of yoga, she knew me well and had

been gently reaching out to me for many years. I would even

venture out to say, Yoga has been calling to me my whole entire life. And though I now found myself in a world surrounded by trauma and chaos, I had been unconsciously living yoga. She was now calling me back home.

In 2018 I was beginning my 20th year in education. I had just re-entered the K-12 classroom as a High School Intensive Reading Teacher and Leader after taking about three months away from teaching in 2014 to relocate from Houston to Florida and adjust to being a full-time caretaker for my grandparents. Then in 2015, I eased back into secondary education as a literacy coach and later an academic manager; both for alternative education settings and later re-entered the high school sector as a Department Chairperson, Content Lead, and Intensive Reading classroom teacher.

Though I was a lover and student of my craft, a PhD scholar, 2014 Teacher of the Year recipient, passionate advocate, teacher mentor, and veteran educator, I struggled. I found myself in a place surrounded by newness and plagued by both inner and outer conflict; and as design would have it, a uterus full of fibroids.

I do not know about anyone else's experience with uterine fibroid tumors, but as a classroom teacher, not free to go to the restroom or tend to my personal needs while hemorrhaging, living with uterine fibroid tumors as a classroom teacher was debilitating. There are at least four notable occasions where I bled completely through my clothes. The constant balance of physical pain, emotional distress, and outside conflict was unbearable. The only way I knew how to show up was fully and I did not have the strength—neither physically, mentally, or emotionally—to show up for myself and my students. This was not a familiar place for me and I needed help. For me, emotional support came in on the wings of yoga.

The Intensive Training was transformational and I felt amazing. I felt as though weights had truly been lifted from me. I underwent surgery, emotional surgery. I was so excited about my healing and experience during my yoga training, I made the common mistake of wanting to share this good news with everybody. The only problem was this: I really did not fully understand what had happened. My foundation was not yet secure. But I was on a yoga high. When I was still fully in the smoky haze of my yoga high, the founder of Breathe for Change asked if I wanted to join the Breathe for Change team as a facilitator for the DC Yoga Teacher Training that was occurring seven days after my yoga teacher training. A facilitator had dropped out and they were in need of someone to help facilitate a group: "I just love your energy and think you would be a great fit for the team and help for the lead facilitator." I was beyond excited for so many reasons. I wanted to step into the community and share the gift of emotional healing. My vision of both a business and a non-profit had lay dormant for several years, unsure of what to do to really step out with either of these visions and as a reluctant classroom teacher, I wanted a way out. I just knew that this invitation to join the DC Summer 2018 Breathe for Change Facilitator Team was the answer to all my prayers. The pin in the balloon: You cannot tell anyone. Please keep it a secret. Slowly, my rose-colored glasses began to clear: "This is not really how I want to receive this gift," I thought to myself. Yet, I soldiered on. I took a few days for "reflection" and sought the counsel of those closest to me. I came back the next day with a "well thought out" YES! And with no clue of what I was truly saying yes to, and the promise of $1400 stipend pay for eighteen days in DC, paid lodging, a plane ticket, an experience to support sixty-five teachers who would become yoga teachers, and the chance to visit the nation's capital, I said YES. Five days after my yoga teacher training, with the ink still wet on my 200-hour Vinyasa certificate and non-refundable $500 canceled conference registration for a prior commitment, I headed to DC to do Lord knows what.

My DC experience was strikingly different than my Tampa experience. If I could put it in familiar terms—perhaps Light and Shadow, Koshas and Kleshas, Yin and Yang, or Day and Night. I went to Washington, DC training looking to experience or recreate what I had in Tampa only to find myself wanting. What I had not fully realized was that in Tampa I was a seeker and cared for as such. In Washington, DC, I was a healer and expected to fully hold space for others when I was still learning to hold space for myself. The result: Hurting in a place that once healed me. I had conflict, great conflict with my fellow yoga teachers. There were unprocessed emotions deep inside of me that bubbled up to the surface and literally spewed out, all over everyone, but namely my housemates and those leading the retreat. I did, however, manage to take extreme care of those I was charged with caring for. They saw nothing of my internal conflict. They had no idea that the yoga teachers were feuding or that there was mistrust and conflict among us. The teachers in training remained unscathed. But I was a mess. The smokey haze from my Tampa experience was long gone. I had both old and new emotional trauma sitting at the top of my chest and I needed a release. But summer was coming to an end. I whisked away on a weekend tryst in Houston and returned to start my new school year: both more broken and more healed than the year before. I was a complete mess.

I maintained my plant-based eating routine. I entertained questions about what I was doing and how I was living, the impetus behind my new lifestyle. I had no real community. No one in my immediate circle was living yoga. I certainly was not living yoga. I was constantly pouring out. All the time, everywhere, I was giving of myself, and there was none left over for me. Only this time, I knew that I was giving pieces of myself away. I knew that I needed space and I tried desperately to create the community that I needed. I was right in the middle of the ocean trying to build a moat.

Little by little I created little spaces and little places where I could breathe and gather myself, externally. My internal environment remained untouched, but intact, mainly by being nourished. Slowly, even my eating and sleeping regiment began to be compromised and I was sliding quickly down a slippery slope. I let go. I let go to save myself. I quit my job.

Within one month of quitting my job I established Be Well, Friends LLC. My plan was to take time to pour into myself. I had some personal savings, at least a three-month cushion to really "peace" myself back together. I did not follow the direction entirely. And MAGY, (My Adult Gap Year) became even more stressful and stress filled than the stress I encountered during my 9-to-5, my W-2 job. I knew in my head and my heart that I needed A PAUSE. I wrote down what that transition looks like, what I needed and what really helped, assisted, and saved me during these moments of transition. Sometimes I have made the mistake in just adding more things to my plate like a cherry on top, but my wellness walk required a different type of commitment. After reflection, here is my result:

Awareness. Assess your current situation. Accept that this is where you are, and that this is what is occurring with you. Tune into what is going on with you and what brought you to this space. Where is this space? Can you name it? Just sit with this awareness for a while with no pressure to do anything about it. Be aware.

Preparation. Prepare yourself and gather what you need; even if the gathering is simply a more mental preparation than a physical one. This is equally important. Coming to terms with the context of what is occurring and mentally preparing ourselves is just as important as physical preparation. Our mentality will bolster us when physical restraints are present. Physical preparation can be as simple as making a listing, clearing our schedule, establishing a routine, or asking for help.

Action. Action plans require movement, whereas preparation does not have to be tangible. Our action is doing something with what we now realized in our previous reflection or meditation time.

Understanding. Understanding acts as both a noun and verb here. Understand that whatever you are doing is new, so allow yourself to have a beginner's mind. Extending compassion and gentleness with ourselves is paramount to embracing new things. This same understanding is to be extended to those in our circle and other networks. Understanding that not everyone will "get" what is going on with you. Understanding that allies may be hard to come by or that people may want to show up, but they do not know how. Understanding that no one can give you complete direction. Understanding that your peace and healing is your responsibility, but there is a myriad of support. The support may be outside of your usual supportive networks, so widen your lens. Understanding that there is a need to be open and flexible, yet focused on your original intention.

Support. Support your own self. Discover your streams of support. Find additional support and supportive networks that you need to start, maintain, and sustain this wellness practice. Support comes in many forms and locations. Thanks to the expansion of the internet and the connected fabric of this vast universe, support does not only mean people we know. Support is ancestors; Activists, past and present. Support is anyone who identifies with your intention and cause and is willing and capable of assisting in caring out your vision. The larger the vision, the more people needed to hold the weight of it. Let yourself be great.

Education. Educating ourselves constantly about this vision, task, situation, or industry to become our own subject matter expert. What are the tenets or the foundation of what we are seeking to accomplish? What is already known and proven that I need to add to my knowledge base? When we fully educate ourselves first by researching and answering our own questions, we are better prepared to withstand criticism and conflict that is sure to come. Until we are able to maneuver through our creating of A PAUSE with complete ease and peace, we are not really ready to share this with the world in detail. This process is solitary. In this part of the journey, there is only room for one person on the road and that is you. Even in the presence of other people, the first entrance into the space is for us, then for others, and lastly, for the rest of the world and larger society.

10
QUIETING THE NOISE

My life is loud, whether within or without, it is blaring. My dad is one of twelve children whose father married a woman with six children of her own, that is a combined eighteen children right there, just with immediate family, not even factoring in his extended. Our McEwen family reunions are mini conventions. I come from a lineage of Baptist preachers—Mississippi Baptist preachers—so we are *loud*. We laugh loud. We talk loud. Pray loud. Argue loud. We are loud.

My mother comes from a smaller immediate family. She is the only girl with four brothers, two older and two younger. My mother's side comes from Louisiana. Her father often shared that he later moved the family to Chicago so that he could "own something". My grandfather was one of nine siblings, and my grandmother was one of seven. But this side of the family is also loud and expressive. We sing and joke, and "hold court" while everyone gathers around for a good story. It's what we do, what we have always done. This side is teachers and singers, and farmers and plant workers, but also natural entertainers. There is also incarceration, substance use and mental health conditions. My mom is the one who made it out. She did not do so unscathed. None of us did. There is no way to survive in this society without scars; even if those scars do not surface until much later in life or show up in different ways. Sociologists and psychologists call them Adverse Childhood Experiences (ACE). When the effects of your childhood activities, environment, encounters and experiences creep into your adult life impacting decision making, well-being, and livelihood.

I believe we are all impacted in some way by our childhoods. Bynum, Freud, Piaget, Maslow, and Erikson were not far off in their assumptions and connections between stages of development in childhood and adolescence and adult evolution and wholeness. Dr. Joy DeGruy correctly turns our attention to some trauma that is passed down through generations, some unknown to us all. Knowing this to be true for me is not a sense of blame or shame, but a sense of awareness. Every adult in some way is healing the wounds of their childhood, no matter how wonderful and perfect. There are just aspects of childhood that we do not even comprehend until adulthood. I personally did not have the language as a child that I now have as an adult to both process and communicate what I am feeling.

Aside from the loudness of my environment, I have always had an inner blaring that I could not turn off. At times in my life, the inner noise has been so loud that I could not hear my own thoughts or decipher them. I was paralyzed. I remember standing in between the pews at church a few years after being discharged from the hospital, and I simply could not move. I could not move because I could not decide where to go or what to do. I was truly perplexed. It seemed like everyone else was so certain. The first church service was over and there was a second to come. Everyone else had scurried off into their cliques to link up at the local Shipley's donuts or whatever other eatery they chose or someone's house, and I felt that I had no one.

I had a roommate that I was not getting along with—I did not like her at the time. She didn't really like me either. We were the best of friends once and now we could not stand each other. I had friends there from college who were in the Christian sorority I pledged, but those friendships were also not standing the test of time. We were loosely connected. I thought that I was perceived to be the crazy one so I allowed myself to slowly fade away.

The congregants were grouped up. I was standing there in the pews alone, reeking with the stench of depression, anxiety and confusion and my insides were loud as a diesel engine. I was an empty shell. I was pretty on the outside but bleeding out on the inside. I was screaming, but no one could hear me because I was desperately trying to quiet the noise. I was quieting the noise by pretending that it was not even loud. That denial only turned up the volume.

As I stood there in between the pew, dripping with uncertainty and paranoia, my only friend from college that I spoke to regularly came to me, "Tamia, you are going to have to do something about this depression." She spoke candidly. "You keep pushing people away and they are not going to want to be around you. That's why nobody wants to be around you...they can feel it." I know she meant well. But that unsolicited criticism broke me. I was already a broken vessel; that was the final blow. TKO. I went home alone. I separated from that friend. I left that church. I found the volume to my inner speaker and learned to adjust the noise and even settle into it a bit. I became okay with moments of loneliness. I learned that appeasing people does not work well for me. I whittled down to nothing and rose back up like a Phoenix. I gained 58 pounds, and then I lost it all. I earned two Master's degrees and a PhD. I became campus and district

teacher of the year. I pledged a beloved sorority graduate chapter. I

held leadership positions at my job. I bought a house. I sold a house. I

won a cruise. I fell in love. I fell out of love. I grew my locs to my butt. I

cut my locs completely off. I died my hair. I went to South Africa,

Botswana, and Zambia and studied abroad. I spoke to a sea of South

African High School children. I visited an orphanage made for children

impacted by Aids in South Africa. I stood outside of Nelson and Winnie

Mandela's homes. I sat inside of Nelson Mandela's jail cell. I sat inside

of Wandee's restaurant and sang with the elders, songs of glory and

victory. I stood on the cliff of Victoria Falls and let the drops of the

waters from this wonder of the world mist my face. I went on Safari in

the South African bush, shared a meal at sunrise with fellow scholars

out of the back of an open-air jeep. I saw a lion and lioness mate. I

saw an elephant protect her young from impending doom. I saw a

beautiful giraffe peak its head through the Zambia trees. I bathed

under the stars in a roofless shower of the South African Chobee game

lodge. I watched the sun rise in the beautiful South African bush, next

to an open-air jeep, waiting to break bread with fellow scholars. All of

these things I did in both expressions of who I believed I was and in defiance of who that friend and others said I was. But it was also in

search of who I was and who I could be.

11

TRIGGERED

I knew that I needed to take a different approach in my life when the day was not washing away at night. I felt sticky. The emotions from each encounter began to compound. It was sticky and was not going away. Each day I got up, I seemed to still be carrying all of the emotions, pain and disappointments from every other day before me. I felt heavy, emotionally heavy. I was confused because I thought I had passed this part of my journey, that I had already successfully learned how to deal with difficult situations and heavy emotions. But what I was now facing felt different, an unfamiliar frightening heaviness that would not wash away at the end of each day. This was with all the lessons I had learned since the initial onset of a full psychosis twenty years earlier as a first-year teacher. This was later after working my wellness plan through mood balancing medication, personal boundary setting, and psychotherapy. This was later still after adapting a plant-based lifestyle and making additional adjustments in my life. This was still as a conscious minded yoga, meditation, qigong teacher and wellness provider with a plant-based eating lifestyle. Things get sticky. The practice of yoga is there to get unstuck, as a reminder that we can wash away the day or simply hold it dear and nurture it and remain in peace.

I was a carefree child. I remember loving life and just being a bright light. I loved to laugh and dance, talk and sing, tell jokes, do impressions, draw, and color. I also loved sports. I was a Liberal Arts brainchild. Anything that involved creativity and self-expression was my area to shine. I loved performing. Creating and performing came naturally. I remember being extremely sensitive to critique and criticism at a very young age. Criticism, critique, or penetrating questions about "Why I was the way I was" caused some emotional distress and I internalized the feedback and shut down. As far as other people were concerned, I guessed that their opinions of me, if negative, should elicit some sort of shut down on my part. I believe this is because even at a young age my actions came from a pure and genuine place and what I wanted most was a genuine, authentic connection with other people. I believe that truly connecting with and relating to others has been a lifelong struggle of mine, being trapped in my own mind, thoughts, or emotions.

Feb 20, 2019 marked 22 years in education for me. I was in the classroom again for the second year in a row after having stepped away for three years to take on leadership roles outside of the classroom, and on Feb. 20, 2019, I grabbed my purse right at the end of 5th period and I left. I quietly gathered my personal items, secured the computers in the classroom to ensure they were out of reach of the students, made sure the room was tidy, locked the door behind me and left. I never came back. I sent an email to the assistant principal, lead administrator in charge at the time that read, "I need to go home. I have a medical emergency." This was sent at the end of 5th period. By the beginning of 6th period, I had secured everything, locked the door behind me, and instructed the students to wait quietly outside the door because someone will be with them momentarily. I kept my composure the best way I knew how.

When I got in my car, I broke down and sobbed uncontrollably the entire way home. I knew I was not coming back, that my 22 years in education had come to an abrupt, unfortunate end. I could not keep up. The rapidly changing pace of education, the many different directions of curriculum and pedagogy and cutting edge research, the classroom trauma both diagnosed and undiagnosed, the racial unrest in the world, the school shootings, the evaluations and strained

relationship with my immediate supervisor and colleagues, the

conflicts with students cursing me out either directly or indirectly, the

destruction of property and classroom materials that I purchased with

my own money, the unpredictable temperatures in the classroom

from frigid to blistering hot, the unsanitary environments and

searching for a 'decent' restroom to use in 10 minutes and rushing

back to the classroom, the multiple accommodations for learning,

language, behavioral and emotional needs as well as cultural, the

deadlines and lesson planning, the loneliness and isolation, the

criticism and feeling of failure—constant failure—and my own

personal, medical, mental, physical and emotional battles being

played out in plain sight, daily, because I had used all of my sick days.

There were 60 days of school left and I would not be getting any more

sick days. There was no way I could earn any more. It was impossible. I

had a plan in place, had filed paperwork for the Family Medical Leave

Act (FMLA), which was guaranteed with my qualifying medical

condition: diagnosed bi-polar disorder. I had planned to work 10 more

days before taking my leave. I had spoken to administrators about my

struggles and need for break. I need intermittent breaks. A respite.

Impossible for a classroom teacher. Even though I knew my time was

coming to an end, I wanted to leave more gracefully and not in a

hailstorm.

That day, Feb 20, I had arrived late. I was not feeling well. I

wanted to call off but felt bad. I forced myself to go to work. My

colleague who was also my content planning partner was on

mandatory leave. She had a nervous breakdown during the school

day. The kids recorded it and uploaded it to their social media sites. I

was barely clinging on. Struggling to come to work daily, painfully

aware that that incident could have easily been me. I could have been

the star of the "snap" with my lowest moment being other people's

amusement. My distress being whispered about in corners by fellow

colleagues, my humiliation being shared for shits and giggles just to

make everyone else feel better that they were not me. I was my

colleague 22 years ago. Only, my students did not have social media;

so it was not captured on video to be shared to reach 1 million views.

However, I was the topic of gossip and object of pity. I was marked as

worthless. Weak. Unable to cope. Can't cut it. Done. First year

teaching and I was cracked wide open. This is where I learned that I

was fragile. I could break. I spent the next 22 years tip toeing and whispering, handling with kit gloves because I did not want to break myself again. This looming awareness of my vulnerability hovered over me, with me wondering always, "Is today the day that I break again?" It escalated to, "Is today the day that I die?" So, on Feb 20, 2019, I left. I left to find a space where I could be human.

How will I know that I have arrived? Follow the path of peace. What I have realized is that I can align with the natural process and seasons. Just like we have seasons in nature, as a part of nature, there are seasons in my life. My goal is to ease into the season and adjust accordingly. Just as in nature, there is seed time and harvest. I will be greatly disappointed if I try to reap during the planting season or plant during harvest time. My prayer is being able to tune into the season; that I may be able to adjust accordingly. Let me be aware and properly equipped with what I need for the season. The Word says that you provide seed for the sower. I trust the provider, provision, and the process. This journey is not to do what others expect, but to live out the truth of my life's purpose.

I created Be Well, Friends. LLC as a model and message of living wellness as our purposes so we do not die on the vine of advocacy. So much about philanthropy speaks of pouring out, but not nearly enough speaks of pouring into our own vessels and only giving from our overflow. This is a remembrance that if I am not overflowing, I have nothing to give. My mission is to fill my cup first. I read numerous articles written about activists, humanitarians, mothers, fathers, Good Samaritans, pastors, and teachers dying while seeking to do good. I was on the fast track to having the same fate. The weight of the world is heavy and we are paying with our lives. If not physical deaths, then certainly emotional, mental, financial, and even spiritual ones. We are losing relationships, career opportunities, inspiration and money by not being well. We still give even when we are depleted. It is time, beyond time to stop this pattern. I must admit, it has been and still is a terribly hard habit for me to break; even as I admonish others. But I am committed to doing life differently. If my industry was not going to prioritize my wellness, my humanity, then I would walk away and create a space where I could be human. A space to help us all Be Well.

First, I have to admit that I am still on the journey, myself, and do not have everything figured out. The first step was to pause and let my breath bring me back to the present moment. There are things I know to be true. It is these truths that center me, apart from any Dharma or streamlined belief system. I must follow the path of peace that resonates with me. When the dust settles and I let go of the status quo, stop being who I thought I should be or think I have to be, what is left is my humanity. I desire to be free to be human, to love and be loved. To live free of excessive suffering, to have my basic needs met and do my part to help meet the needs of others, holding space where I am able to do so.

During my yoga teacher training, the Sanskrit song and chant "Lokah samastah sukhino bhavantu" resonated with me. In English it translates to, "May all beings be well and may my words, thoughts and actions contribute in some way to this well-being." That is my truest heart sentiment. I can simply drop in the names of those I know, like, and care about and lastly, humanity as a whole, because this prayer is for all beings. It includes the environment, animals, my neighbors, my family, my friends and me. May we all be well and may all of our words, thoughts, and actions contribute in some way to this well-being.

When I walked away from a profession that I had loved

fiercely for 22 years, it was not out of anger or even sadness as I

stated in earlier writings. It was from the purest place of love that I

knew. I wanted to be better, not perfect. Just better. I wanted to be in

a place where I could respond from a place of love, not lack. A place of

joy, not envy and resentment. A place of peace, not pride. I needed to

create space for my own humanity, to be broken and confused and

heartsick without projecting that pain and conflicting emotions on

others. This needed to be done in a secret place. A sacred space that

was not before everyone else's eyes. I quit my job, so others would

not have to. I quit my job so I could heal, so I could have space to be

human and give others that same space.

During my time away, I saw the need to also disconnect from

my social networks, my family in ways that they did not understand.

These were ways that I did not understand. But it made sense. I had

no clue what was happening with me on the inside, I needed solitude

to let that inner work be done. I am grateful for the gift of space. The

mind. The body. The spirit. These all know how to heal and repair

themselves, but we must give them space to do so. Space not overfull

with agendas and deadlines. Space not clouded with toxins and processed food. Space not piled high with rigid belief systems and

fixed mindsets. But space filled with stillness, the beauty of nature, the

nourishment of plants, the grace of gentleness and creativity. Space

for humanity.

Ashe'

Maybe I should have known that the Universe was bracing me for the coming impact. Perhaps if I had paid closer attention to when the random passerby attacked my car, kicking it forcefully until the driver's door was dented shut, screaming, "Nigger Bitch!"; or the impatient mom of three children parked behind me at the Walgreen's Pharmacy window who honked and demanded I move out of line to let her out because her "babies gotta pee", I would have seen this as the omen that it really was for my time ahead in Florida and society as a whole. Me politely motioning for her to back up, instead, because I was at the window and feared moving and losing my place, unable to fill my prescription before Walgreen's closed. I needed my medicine. I would be driving 16 hours to Florida the next morning to relocate. I couldn't risk going to this new place without my medication and possibly spaz out in a new environment. What then? I was not going to taint this new beginning with remnants of an old disjointed me. Nope, I would show up in Florida and brave this new frontier with a clean slate. Not only will nobody know my name. Nobody will know my baggage. I am free to craft the narrative of my choice.

I was a master sculptor. Not that I was prone to lying, but I certainly knew how to shed old skin. I paid no real attention to this angry mother who cursed me, "Fucking lazy nigger!" when I would not move up to let her out of line. I paid even less attention when after we both received our drive through window prescriptions, I pulled off to the side, got out of my car, then walked within view just enough to capture her license plate number. "I'll file a report", I thought. "She can't just verbally assault me like that and use racial slurs." My house of 11 years was packed up in boxes. Among my items, the 2014 Spring Independent School District Secondary Teacher of the Year Award alongside my Caribbean cruise for two: I was an upstanding citizen, pillar of the community. As I walked back to my car, adjusted my seat and began the reporting process, I asked myself, "Is this really an emergency? Should I call 911 or 311? Am I inside or outside the city limits?" My internal dialog was broken by her, the angry mom wedging my car in, blocking my path to bid me ado with a final "lazy ass nigger". She was Latina. I was Dr. Tamia A. McEwen, 2014 Spring Independent School District Secondary Teacher of the Year. Apparently, I was a lazy ass nigger, too.

By the time I made my incident report, was rerouted to another precinct and made it home to finish packing, an officer was dispatched to my house. Apparently, the angry mother made her phone call quicker than me. The officer was coming to question me because she falsely reported me, ME, for using racial slurs at HER. I did no such thing. But she got through first, so it was my Black lazy ass nigger word against hers. Me, the antagonist and instigator, apparently.

I was an unstable lit match and had the anti-psychotic medication in hand to prove it. Right? Wrong. In fact, I was never actually that person. I only feared that I could become that person. There I stood in my doorway, interrogated by an officer who questioned my character and sense of dignity, while my boxed achievements looked on at the mockery of it all. Slowed by anxiety and internal conflict, I did not reach the precinct office first. The officer questioned my ethics. I questioned my sanity. He left. I finished packing and headed to Florida to embark on a new venture 0-2.

FRACTURED MIRROR

I had to learn what to do with strong emotions and unpleasant feelings that welled up inside of me; those that seemed not to align with who I believed I was and how I wanted to show up in the world. Some call this Cognitive Dissonance: a reality that clashes with our sense of self, truth, and beliefs or values about ourselves, something or someone dear to us, or the world around us. Previously, I was stressed and unfilled in the classroom, but my bills were paid. I just needed to not be concerned about what people felt or thought about me. I got side-tracked and that took me off course. *Why don't they like me? Why aren't we clicking? I just thought working here would feel different, better.*

I sat across from my Executive Director and program manager after a Quality Assurance Review (QAR) meeting. This was my dream job. I was an Academic Manager, working in my field, the field I had earned my PhD in. It was my dream; or at least what I thought was my dream. As a PhD scholar, you do not always get to work in your research area. Sometimes you do not get a job anywhere near your degree. But this assignment was all about my area of expertise: designing curriculum and guiding instruction.

"The staff is complaining...they don't like you." It was a dagger in my chest. Inwardly I shrank.

Then I stilled myself with, "well, I'm here for the kids, so that's all that matters."

"And..." the Executive Director continued, "The girls don't like you either. They say you are rude."

For a minute my mind went blank. I saw lips moving but heard nothing further. "How?" I thought. I had stayed up late nights, come in early. Bought muffins with my own money, even washed soiled clothing and developed an entire thriving education program. Dejected, I immediately turned to my defenses. "I tender my resignation...effective immediately." I said with even tone and breath.

"Now wait, Dr. McEwen!" I had only been called Tamia or Ms. Tamia with a reluctant Dr. Tamia until this point. "Let's maybe think this through, work around it." I was stone faced. If all I had been and done, even through weariness, was not enough to be seen and accepted without ridicule and being picked a part, this is not the place for me. That was my resolve. Good, bad, or indifferent I did not want to be any place where I was merely tolerated. But the sting on my cracked soul would take longer to ease. Something broke inside of me, and I was not certain it could be repaired.

The gift of journaling, nutrition, meditation, yoga and over all wellness is space to place those emotions, sit with them, and release. I know that I can pour my feelings into a painting or dance routine or yoga practice or meditation session or simply allow nature to revive and comfort me after sitting outside or walking, or standing in the Sun. I know that relationships are gifts. I have made a commitment protect my consciousness, be responsible for the energy that I give and receive, bolster my stability, and not be afraid to abandon the status quo. And to work in spaces that are emotionally safe, centered in a culture of well-being.

12
LAUNCH INTO SPACE

I received a call from a mentee late one evening. Her siblings needed an emergency placement for the night so they could stay together and be transferred to their aunts care the next morning. I agreed after talking it over briefly with two friends. Then I called my mom who was still hazy from sleep. My sister who had been living with me for a few months was out of town, due back in a day or so. My family was set to head to Louisiana to a reunion near the end of the week. Still, I figured, "I can provide a safe haven for the night." I have a three-bedroom condo, plenty of food, and a supportive network. Though I hesitated briefly, and went through all the necessary background checks, including disclosing that I do deal with anxiety and depression, two of the three children were released in my care as an emergency placement.

Emergency placements are up to 72 hours, three days. Five days in, I still had the children. My relationship with my immediate family became strained, and the emotional weight unbearable. Confused and concerned for my well-being, they did not agree with my decision. That was the first and only time in my life that I recall my family taking a hands- off approach. "This was your decision. Handle it the best way you can." I was stunned. My sorority chapter members filled in to assist as best they could. They donated money, helped to purchase groceries, and came over to help prepare the house for the arrival of the third child. "Give the kids back" my sister said, each time she called. My immediate family had never been involved with the system. We had never been in the system or taken care of anyone else who had been. This was a line we never crossed as a family.

Personally, my energy levels started to drop. I was not sleeping fully. I was not eating as I used to. My days were split between being on the phone speaking with Health Care representatives, establishing a safe routine for the kids, and explaining to or dodging questions from my family about what I was doing. My self-care routine had been altered. We established a good routine at the house: 8pm bedtime with a 1pm-2pm built in quiet time that could be a nap, reading a book, sitting quietly or just relaxing without the tv or electronics; all-natural foods with no processed food or sugar since the children had emotional and physical needs.

My money was getting thin and patience thinner. Still the kids were well cared for and in good health and spirits. I was declining. My crying spells were returning. Thursday, my family left for the family

reunion in Louisiana. Then came Friday. I received a call that the third

child would arrive that evening. A bed was delivered, donated by a

local charity. Sorority Chapter members came over to help prepare the

spare room for the third child. They did their best, but the nighttime

routine had been disturbed. I started to panic. "Can someone just stay

over tonight, so I can get some sleep? With the third child to arrive

soon, I don't feel comfortable being here alone with my being so

exhausted and the kids still being up with me not knowing the third

child yet and not knowing how they will interact with each other. I just

need some help tonight and some rest." No one could stay. I broke

out in tears once I realized that no one could stay. It was not my usual

response, but I was at the end of my emotional rope. I overheard

someone say, "She is not mentally and emotionally prepared enough

to handle these kids." My heart broke. It was not that. I just needed

rest. I needed for those who truly loved and cared for me to just help a

little while longer with these specifics: turn down the lights, give the

kids a bath, help do hair, keep the conversation down, and let me rest.

It is difficult to clearly articulate your needs when you are in the

middle of a situation and at the end of your emotional reservoir.

I made the request, but no one could do it. That was not possible. People were not willing to do that, not out of spite. They just did not see the necessity of providing that type of support. I articulated it the best way I could. They said that I had to give the kids back. That I had to tell the investigative supervisor that I did not want the kids. I wanted the kids and would provide a safe haven for them, but I needed a nap. Since I could not get them both, I had to give the kids back. "Tamia, when he rings that doorbell you have to tell him in these very exact words... 'I am unable to care for the kids. Take them back.' Do you understand me?" Spoken to me in slow, low tones as though I was the child. Both my pride and my spirit were wounded. I wept. It was more like a whimper because I did not want the kids to hear me or see me crying. I wiped my tears and began to pack the kids' items. They came to me with soiled clothes and a princess video. I packed their items in a duffle bag that I had received from an educational conference. I boxed their toys, books, and donated clothes and obliged in letting them take a whole jar of pickles that they requested to take with them. "You are going to get a chance to all stay together" I said to the children, holding back tears. When the doorbell rings, you will be leaving with the inspector." The children were excited about being able to stay together as siblings and take all their things with them. I, on the other hand, was destroyed on the inside.

Late Friday night, the doorbell rang. It was the Investigative Supervisor to pick up the children. My mind quickly turned to the conversation we had earlier in the day. I had tried my best to explain to the Investigative Supervisor what I needed as support. He kept asking, "Ms. McEwen, are you saying that you don't want the kids?" I was so confused. That is not what I was saying at all. "I don't have the support I thought I would have, so I cannot keep the kids any longer. Please take them with you and see to it that they stay together." We hung up the phone.

It was now near midnight. I turned the knob. The investigator stood in the doorway with a visibly tired 11year old. I smiled, and motioned to sit down and eat pizza with the other siblings that were still awake, way past our established bedtime. They all hugged and greeted each other. I handed over all of their belongings, old and new. After eating, they skipped off to the car with the Investigative Supervisor. "Bye auntie! Thank you, auntie! We love you, auntie!" I gave them the remaining box of pizza. "No eating in the car." The investigative supervisor gently admonished them. "Thank you so much...Ms. Ummm Whachumacallit! Bless you Ms—" the third child paused "Ms___what's your name again?" "Ms. Tamia!" The other two called out. "Bless you Ms. Tamia." The third child offered a correction. "Y'all, put on your seat belts and sit back." The third child's role as 11year old protector had resumed. They drove away.

My house, now quiet. A child's bed sat in my former office. Traces of smuggled Nerds candy and Fruit snacks aligned the floor in different spots. I said my goodbyes to my sorority sisters that came over to assist. They did their best. I waved goodbye to them all. I laid in bed and tried to rest from the whirlwind of the prior week's events. I wept instead of going to sleep. My house was quiet, but my mind was loud. Everyone was gone and now I had to sit with all that had bubbled up during these past few days. My family was still out of town, scheduled to return in a few days. I still was not sleeping. Phone calls about the children from their extended family: Where are they? We want them! I felt powerless. I did not know the system well enough, and apparently, I did not know people well enough, either.

Mentally, physically, and emotionally I was declining. The guilt. The confusion. The feelings of abandonment and loss. The lack of confidence in my decision-making skills. The lack of sleep. The hopelessness. The embarrassment. The paranoia. The mistrust. The delusions started. The hallucinations came back. The fear of, "what if something happens to the children? Paranoia set in, "I never should have said yes." Every question from my family and friends was now coming back to visit me at night when I tried to sleep. People were having conversations about me, but I had no clue what they were saying. I knew what I needed. I spoke many times over, but no one heard me. Conversations with my family turned into a one-way channel. I could tell that their conversation with me developed from a conversation that they had about me without me: I did not like it.

I could feel that they had a plan and was going to institute the plan with or without my consent. It made me nervous, paranoid, livid and broke my heart at the same time. If my actions in any way made them uncomfortable to the point where they felt like I was a danger to myself or someone else, I could be "Baker Acted", held involuntarily against my will. In Florida, a Baker Act is the social, political, and financial death knoll, the proverbial pin in the cushion; the nail in the coffin for a person living with a mental health condition. I was terrified

at the possibility of being Baker Acted. My ability to maintain a cool

pleasant disposition was my only saving grace. I had several

conversations with myself: "Tamia, you have to remain calm. If you

become aggressive or irate, people are only going to see a crazy, angry

Black woman. You will immediately become a threat. Whatever you

do, do not resist. Just comply and only speak when you are calm

enough to do so. God has got you. The Universe has your back." I sat

back and I wept. Most times I cried because I was speaking, but not

being heard. The tears became my communication with God. Each

time I cried it was a release and a clarion cry for help. Through breath

and through tears my help came in.

My parents did have a plan. Their plan was to have a Peer

Specialist meet and speak with me and the family about an

intervention plan and local services through the National Alliance on

Mental Illness (NAMI) offered called PEER Support. What neither my

family, nor the PEER specialist knew, was that I had sought out local

services. I had been to NAMI Network of services page and even

reached out to a NAMI representative before I resigned from my job

to seek guidance and assistance with the conflicts I was facing. That turned into yet another hurdle coupled with more questions. One

thing that I had always been is an advocate for myself. Whether it was

telling the cousin to "stop bothering me, I'm trying to take a nap" at

the age of two years old, or asking for space and quiet time at forty-

two, I have always been my own advocate; even if I forgot or chose

the long and winding road of advocacy. As for the children, I did not

have any further contact with the children or their guardians, but I did

receive updates that they were together and doing well. My focus had

to return to building back up my emotional and physical wellness. I

pray for them often.

The first time I reached out to the state NAMI representative, the

person said that there was nothing that could be done to assist me in

my situation. This time, as a family we got connected to the local

NAMI affiliate. I began to attend PEER support sessions and re-

institute my tools of resiliency. I attended a NAMI conference. I

appeared on the Breakfast Club to share my mental health journey

and testimony of mental wellness and physical healing through a

plant-based lifestyle and going through the HOPE Beyond Fibroids

Elimination Program with Drs Amsu, Amun, Chef Ahki and Coach

Gessie in 2018. But it was not over yet. I had not "arrived". I am still and will always be on the path of healing and thriving because this life

of healing and living victoriously depends on daily choices. The choices

I make each day determine how much "coast and glide time I will

have." Anyone who has ever ridden a bike, or operated any manual

moving system, knows that there are moments and points where you

must pump or peddle. Then there are moments and conditions where

you can coast or glide. Different terrain requires a different technique

or force. My decline from this experience reminded me just how much

my lifestyle was my stabilizing and saving grace. I lived my way into my

condition, and I would have to live my way out. My balance of

meditation, emotional release, loving spaces, nutritious food, and

quality sleep is my self-care plan. I must be mindful not to frivolously

move the pegs around.

I connected with NAMI peer support and consistently attended

PEER group sessions. I looked for a local yoga community where I

could regularly practice. I found a Qigong class instead. The yoga class

had a "lock the door" policy and late arrivals could not enter. On this

day, I was a late arrival. I took up Qigong and started learning about

energy work. Through the moving meditation series, I learned that I

could pull my energy back in and send it out. I could respond instead of react and breath is continuously my guide through all things. I was slowly coming back to myself. I took the instructor's course for that, as well. After 1 years' practice and self-study, 110 Direct Instruction hours with Master Qigong Instructor, John Walcott, The Cloudwalker, I received my Level 1 Qigong certificate. This is a lifestyle, not a profession.

Slowly I started to build myself back up. I leaned on my practice to pull me back and keep me standing strong or help me to lay down and surrender to the process of life. I sat in meditation online with Faith Hunter for 30 Days. I obtained a Yoga mentor through Black Yoga Teacher Alliance (BYTA), Denise Alston, a veteran yoga teacher. We met bi-weekly for three months, speaking for about an hour each session to just check in on one another. She helped me to start building my confidence back up as a yoga instructor. She also helped to put a realistic plan in place for me to grow my wellness business and to be compensated for my craft and expertise. I attended small business sessions given for free through SCORE and the Small Business Development Center (SBDC), that was connected with the local community colleges. I reconnected with other wellness professionals in the area and yoga teachers from my two trainings in Tampa and DC.

I built a personal yoga practice by watching Mark Whitwell, the Heart of Yoga. I became intentional about my own personal practice and just started with daily sun salutations for 40 days. That was the charge from Heart of Yoga, and it completely changed my practice inside and outside. I began to study and focus more about nutrition versus do's and don'ts of meals and food groups. I came across research about trauma and the brain, foods for brain health, foods for mental health, the connection between inflammation and psychiatric disorders and the blood tests that can detect inflammation in the body and brain as well as protein in the blood, which is an indication of brain inflammation. I visited a chiropractor to get spinal adjustments and got regular massages through his office to help alleviate stress. The next few months I returned to receive a nutritional assessment and four weeks of recommended vitamins through hydration therapy to raise my iron and vitamin levels. The doctor complemented me on how well I am taking care of myself. It all seemed so simple and can be traced back to one question, "What does it mean to be well?"

"Health equity means that everyone has a fair and just opportunity to be as healthy as possible. This requires removing obstacles to health such as poverty, discrimination, and their consequences, including powerlessness and lack of access to good jobs with fair pay, quality education and housing, safe environments, and health care."

-Robert Wood Johnson Foundation

Wellness must be accessible, obtainable, sustainable, responsive, and comprehensive in order to truly stick. For me to embrace a lifestyle of wellness beyond following a diet fad for a few days, a perspective change was critical and paramount. In order for that lifestyle of wellness to be sustained, a culture of well-being is critical at the institutional level.

When we are well, we are able to better relate to others and together we can do the work of creating the culture of well-being, through community, that we desire. Communities and societies do not build themselves. They are the collective formations of individuals. Because we are all on this journey at different phases, our roles will vary. The more individual and collective healing we have, the more we will see our families and communities transform because we are now

operating from a well-being centered mindset.

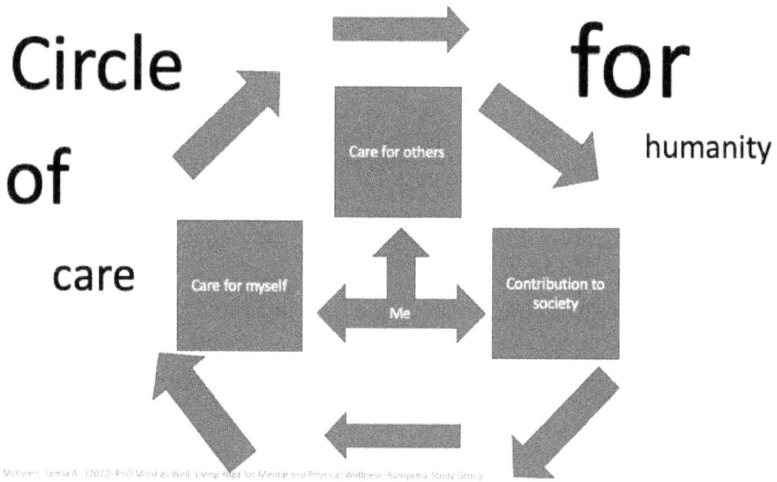

Circle of care for humanity

Care for others

Me

Care for myself

Contribution to society

PART THREE

RECOVERY

13
BE WELL, FRIENDS

I say be well friends because that is my true Heart sentiment. When I think of my own journey it really began with me wanting my feelings to match up with my truest intention. There would be days that I would desire to be active, happy and engaging, but I just could not get all of the parts of me to line up and show up in the world in that way. I remember distinctly standing in the middle of the pews after a church service, seeing all of the people milling around— laughing, hugging, interacting with each other with so much ease. And there I was feeling like a prisoner in my own body and my own mind.

On top of my own internal imprisonment, I heard the criticism of others: "Why do you look like that? What's wrong with you? Cheer up! Or, "You know what? When you come around like that it makes people not want to be around you...one of these days you are going to push people away so far and there is not going to be anyone left but you. You are going to be all alone." I felt like a prisoner because I wanted to be a part of that interaction. I wanted to smile and hug and wave at people and be able to socialize with ease and freedom, but something inside of me was terrified to do so, and then other parts of

me just did not want to do it. At times there was just fiery rage that

boiled up inside of me. I was irritable and short tempered. Impatient

and intolerant. Hopeless and helpless but also wanting. I wanted a

sense of stillness. I wanted to be love. I wanted to be light.

I stood there that day in the middle of the church pews, simply

frozen in place with my mind traveling back to thoughts of being

admitted to a mental facility. As I watched these people mill around, I

could not help but think how different their lives were from mine.

There were at least 200 people in that church building. Research

shows that 1 in every 4 women experience sexual assault and 1 in 5

people have a mental health condition. By this calculation between 40

or 50 other people could relate, but I was not aware of this. I was in

the midst of people, yet still so very alone. Invisible. Hiding in plain

sight.

Even though I had graduated college with a Bachelor of

Science degree in Psychology, had studied and learned about the mind

and even the body and how the two work together, I still was not

completely aware of my own mind body alignment, inner workings or what it meant to live and be well. I lived my life the way I had learned

to live it and studied theories, case studies, and people without

making a true direct connection with myself. I was an expert at seeing

signs in other people, but the whole complete connection to myself,

my own awareness, remained distant. Even though I was rather

introspective and reinvented myself all of the time, I did it in

fragments: I only committed myself to a project up to a certain point

before moving on to something new.

When I spent that one week in the mental health facility,

admitted against my will, I was given mood balancing medication, was

strapped down onto a stretcher upon admittance, and enrolled into

group therapy. My assigned psychiatrist explained all of the symptoms

of psychosis: Acute schizophrenia brought on by stress, followed by bi-

polar disorder type II. And it was at that time that I really saw my

personal, secret silent struggle explained in terms by another person.

My reality was still a bit hazy. I had so many questions. I saw the

condition as temporary and was ready to just "get back to normal". I

would then spend nearly 20 years hiding underneath the cloak of

shame that can come with the stamp of mental health condition. I

would spend over twenty years de-stigmatizing, learning to talk nice to myself again. My inner critic blaring: You are broken. You are

incomplete. You are crazy.

I have met with mental health professionals directly during three critical times in my life: Mental Health Crises, Mental Health Maintenance, Mental Health Recovery. During the first visit the psychiatrist diagnosed me, in the second visit the psychiatrist treated me, in the third visit the psychiatrist released me and even questioned me, "Why are you still here?" It was almost as if I was a caged bird that needed to be set free, that needed to exit the same way I entered. A psych eval brought me on this journey and I somehow needed a psych eval to lead me out and convince me of my freedom. There is power in prevention, of having a mental health check in before crises sets in to just Check in with our own selves to see how we are doing emotionally.

During my stay in in-patient care in 1998, I attended group classes and met with a psychiatrist regularly to learn basic lifestyle wellness strategies and establish daily routines. I learned them enough to be released within one week and to maintain my own routine outside of the hospital. I did not come across a comprehensive explanation of phases of psychosis until twenty years later. Looking back on that experience I can now clearly see times in my life where I was in various stages of psychosis and might still experience certain remnants every now and then. The difference is awareness and knowledge, and acceptance of any state of mind in which I may be. It is making peace with my entire mind.

The National Institute of Health (NIH), and the National Institute of Mental Health (NIMH) have conducted extensive studies on recovering from a psychotic episode. Their research initiative RAISE (Recovery After Initial Schizophrenic Episode) looks at the importance of having treatment or Coordinated Specialized Care (CSC) after an initial psychosis onset.

Yale Institute of Mental Health Specialized Treatment for Early Psychosis (STEP) program breaks down the stages of psychosis into three phases: Prodrome, Acute, and Recovery. What I came to learn is that the length of the phases can last many years. It is not just a single event and then it is over. There are lifestyle change interventions that can be implemented to during each stage to prevent a full psychosis onset. There is a level of holistic health care that is needed to make sure we all stay well: self-awareness and acceptance, trust-worthy and healthy relationships, quality rest, balanced meals with leafy green vegetables and gut healing nutrients, emotional care, and whole life support. After a full psychosis does occur, as in my case, there is the recovery phase. Once we reach the recovery phase and are actively working on our wellness, our very lifestyles that brought us through to recovery are what we must continue to rely on and allow to grow and expand. There will never be a time where I can take an extended break from nutritious food and quality rest. If I do, I am heading towards diseases.

I thought that there was no space beyond being in recovery, not that you ever graduate from benefitting from therapy, support groups or mental health support, but the approach to life's stressors is different. My life after experiencing a total decline and coming out on the other side is different from before that incident and being in that crisis. Being aware of living a thriving and sustainable life of wellness is hope that I never thought was possible. To this realization I say there is always beyond. Rather than reach for it and miss the beauty of the present moments that I am in, I may simply allow it to exist and step into it whenever that time comes, if that time comes.

AN OFFERING

Through yoga I was offered a perspective that aligned with who I believe I truly am: A lover of all things and people who desires to do and be good. I do realize the need for money, capital or wealth to truly be liberated in this world that we live in. With that understanding, I accepted that as I set my intentions, the Universe conspires with me to make it happen. Life is not happening to me. Life is happening with me and because of me, my own expressions, and my own requests. Upon this realization, I became paralyzed with silent fear for a moment, not wanting to "accidentally create something" that I would live to regret. I now offer myself grace and take it moment by moment.

Here is my reality and what I have manifested, that which I am truly proud of. In February 2019, I quit my career of 22 years with about six months' worth of cushion in my savings. Within one month of leaving my salaried job, I established a wellness support business: Be Well, Friends. LLC. A year and some months later, I am still establishing myself in the Wellness arena, but I am well. My bills are paid. My needs are met. We are in a Global Pandemic, over 12 months in now from the entire world shutting down and the economy being at a standstill, and yet, I am well. As a person who has been totally aware of both my fragility and my strength and the power and necessity of life balance and now, mind body balance, wellness has been my life focus even as an unconscious reality. It has been my path. It is my path. Of this I am sure.

What am I doing now? I am a Mental Health and Wellness Advocate and state recognized Mental and Behavioral Health Support Provider through the Peer Coalition Network of Florida and Certified Recovery Peer Specialist (CRPS). This allows me to have a career as a mental wellness advocate under my own foundation and agency. I am partnering with other wellness and mental and behavioral health professionals—along with yoga, qigong and meditation teachers—and we are holding space for ourselves, each other, and our larger communities to heal. And I am resting, sitting in meditation, enjoying my family and eating well. I am taking naps, drinking spring water, eating kale and blue chips and minding my business. It is not the way I envisioned it, but it is the road that is being laid out for me and I am forever grateful.

I will continue to allow the practice of yoga to be my confidant and my guide as I hold space, create space, and share space on this wellness journey.

AN INVITATION

In a recent group meeting of Yoga as a Peace Practice, Black Yoga Teacher Alliance (BYTA) co-founder Jana Long asked us to ponder: What brought you to yoga? She followed by explaining that whatever brought us to yoga determines the path we take. Our reason for coming to yoga will determine what resonates with us and what does not. It will be the guiding factor of what we are drawn to and what drives us away.

I often say that I came to yoga to find a place to "Put my emotions". I had already rebuilt my life and career from a potentially devastating nervous breakdown some twenty-years prior. I was on the road to healing my body from the symptoms of uterine fibroid tumors. I was working full time as a classroom Intensive Reading Teacher and Department Chairperson. My salary was about $25K less than when I lived in Houston, but I was maintaining. My bills were lower: car paid off, eating mostly fresh produce, and I was not hanging out much. My overall cost of living was manageable, so the large salary was not a necessity.

What was plaguing me was emotional turmoil. I had encountered numerous conflicts with people over the years in every network: personal, career, philanthropic. These conflicts were not washing off at the end of the day. My life became a series of starts, stops, start overs, and intermittent encounters that left a carnage of broken relationships. I felt severely disconnected from everyone and everything, even the people that I loved and I knew loved me. This same scenario began to play out in my career. Up until I moved to Florida, I had managed to keep a stable career with a few job changes. Upon moving to Florida, once I started working, those social networks seemed much more difficult to pin down. I could not digest criticism and began to believe that everyone was against me. This went deeper than just issues on the job. I found myself in a place where I did not trust anyone. No relationship I had was untouched by what I believe to be my deep emotional wounds. In short, I felt completely out of balance. On the outside I looked rather well, but my inner peace, or lack thereof, did not match with my outer appearance. I knew that if I did not get a handle on my inner unrest, it would eventually show up in my outer functions. The main places it did show up was in my relationships and my physical wellness. It eventually showed up in my career path. With no space or method to process my emotions, I quit my job in education after twenty-two total years. This was not the form of retirement I envisioned. What it did allow, however, is a platform to fully step into the sphere of wellness. But it was a new space that I was unfamiliar with.

I had twenty-two proven years as a veteran educator. In the wellness spectrum, I only had two years in as a certified yoga and meditation instructor, and less than a month as a Qigong practitioner. I had nearly three years on the scene of living a plant-based lifestyle. The truth is, I felt out of place, unqualified, and unworthy to speak freely in the wellness space. Who am I to tell someone how to be well? What do I know about yoga and Qigong or meditation? I had just gotten this measure of peace. Even more loud within me was the ache of remaining quiet. I could not rest and not share with others what I had learned what had worked for me. I was constantly hearing about the impact of stress on the mind and body and how Black people are disproportionately impacted by lifestyle related illnesses and health concerns. Deep down, I knew that the compounded stress of transgenerational trauma and systemic racism, with mounting societal conflicts and oppression, multiplied the impact for Black people. This is one of the leading reasons Black health concerns are fatal. But I was also completely terrified of failure and criticism. People are not always open or ready to hear anything about changing their lifestyle, and change is not easy. My mind became plagued with worry: the worry of not doing enough vs the worry of doing too much. The practice that healed me was becoming the practice that killed my joy. It would succeed only if I let it and did not stay true to the practice of living yoga, all eight limbs. The practice of yoga is not just fancy poses. The practice of yoga teaches us to sit with those heavy emotions, to let our breath guide us, calm us, energize us and comfort us. Let the practice lead you out of what the practice sometimes leads you into.

And so it was. The practice saved me time and time again. From isolation. From self-criticism. From self-doubt. From ego. From selfishness and greed. From grandiose thinking. From a lack mentality. From inaction. From conflict within. From conflict with others. From excessive compulsion and mania. The practice continues to lead me out. If I only remember to just Be. Then forget and remember again. If we allow her, she will not leave us lacking and astray. The practice is here for life. I call her yoga.

I posted this reflection in the Black Yoga Teacher's Alliance (BYTA) Facebook Group:

What brought you to yoga? For me, it was in 2016 as I was scrolling through FB and saw an ad for Breathe for Change: Yoga teacher certification for educators (trauma based & SEL). Intrigued, I scrolled the website, which seemed to be the holy grail to my inner and outer turmoil. I loved education & life, but I was tired and hurting...everywhere. I sat there, chest heavy from the weight of life: classroom teacher (new state and new pressures), death of both grandparents whom I moved to Florida to help take care of, working to manage my emotions without medication (20-year mental wellness recovery), heavy bleeding from fibroids. I sat there. I requested a training near me and received a response in 2017 that in the summer of 2018 a training would open in Tampa (2hrs away). By then, I had declined a recommended hysterectomy and turned to plant-based eating, seeking to heal my fibroids naturally. I had joined a healing group of sisters who were also fighting to save their uteruses. Yet, I still needed somewhere to put my emotions. Apparently, they had all settled in my womb.

Summer 2018, I met yoga face to face: Sixteen days intensive training and 200 hours later, a sweet hello. I started yoga teacher training about five months into my plant-based eating journey. Yoga opened her arms wide. She guided me with breath. She embraced me and cracked me wide open, in an amazing way. She and I are still rocking together. There is still so much to learn. Beginner's mind. But she is gentle with me and I with her. Today, I still have my mind. I still have my uterus, and I still have yoga. So, if I may ask again, what brought you to yoga?

Love,

Tamia

14
MEDS

It took a little while for me to get adjusted to a life of taking

daily medication. I was a 23-year-old who looked fine on the outside,

but was very fractured on the inside. It was no mystery. There was no

excessively devastating traumatic event or deep seated happening

that fractured me on the inside; it was just how things manifested

internally. I did not know that there was any special care that needed

to be taken for my inner strength. I certainly did not know that there

was a connection between the inside, the outside and my overall

health and wellness. I absolutely had no idea about all of the "selves":

physical, mental, emotional, physiological, spiritual. That lesson would

not be learned until nearly 20 years later during yoga teacher training.

But I learned how to manage this new life of daily doses of

medication, which came with its own set of challenges. Because my

medication had to be taken with food, I learned to set my schedule

around being able to have something on my stomach. This had to be

balanced with eating by a certain time so that the last meal would not

disrupt my sleep. Then I learned that possibly eating a piece a bread or drinking a glass of milk could help settle my stomach, too. These, however, were things unique to me in my friends' circle. This meant it required me to pull away from the group or possibly pack some extra snacks or lay down for naps or leave early from events because staying out late did not fare well with me taking medication. Even after being in in-patient care for one week, I was not able to just pick up and move forward with life as usual. I had a totally new life. I tried to normalize my life, still. I simply tried to sketch myself back into the picture of my old life (choir rehearsal, children's choir, youth group mentor, work, home, etc.), but it was not that easy.

I had monthly meetings with my psychiatrist where I learned about medication management and my new diagnosis: acute schizophrenia. It was explained that my condition was temporary. Because my personality was so gregarious, I was such a likeable person, high functioning, some would say, my inner brokenness was easily masked. Intellectually, I knew all the right things to do and say, but emotionally I had no clue how to execute or make this balance sustainable. I did not know how to juggle all the pins of life: Those on the inside or those on the outside. I simply just dealt with whatever came up on my radar. Therefore, for the next 20 years or so, I was always in motion. I just had medication, a pretty set routine, and a bed time; still in motion.

After about a year in psychotherapy and having stabilized with no other major episodes, I stopped taking my medication. I had gained nearly 70 lbs. and could not keep gaining weight unless I now wanted to deal with diabetes and hypertension on top of psychosis. I remained pretty stable. I got a roommate, one of my friends from college. I re-entered my extra-curricular activities at church: choir, praise dance, children's church, youth mentor, sound ministry, singles group. I kept up with my responsibilities at work: high school English teacher, team leader, testing coordinator, night school teacher, mentor. I got my finances in order: bought a car, had two cars, upgraded apartments, took a financial literacy course, set my budget, bought a house, got two second jobs (group home & adjunct professor at the college). I grew my social circle: started dating again, hung out with friends, joined online dating groups. Over a span of about 10 years, I was back on track. I hit a wall and began to spiral after a few low points that I could not shake. I went into a depressive cycle that lasted about a week and I could not get out of bed to go to work.

I only had a limited amount of time as a classroom teacher, and I feared that I would lose my job. After flipping through a magazine, I saw an advertisement about mood disorders, which read: "When your mood begins to impact your day-to-day activities, you need to seek help." That was precisely what was happening with me. My mood would not allow me to keep the job I had to work at the pace I was committed to work, so I needed some help. I contacted my local physician to make an appointment and was scheduled to see a physician's assistant named Tammy, who gave me a mood questionnaire. This questionnaire asked me questions about things that I did not realize were mood related: racing thoughts? Difficulty concentrating? Plagued by fear? Difficulty sleeping? Emotional outbursts? Yes. Yes. Yes. Yes. Yes. I had checked yes to ALL questions. I left with a diagnosis of bi-polar disorder and sense of freedom.

At least I knew what I was fighting. I could name it. I could call it out and truly fight it. I was not just weird. Something was going on with my brain. Some chemical imbalance was the root cause. Knowing this somehow gave me solace. It was not the whole story, however. The remaining days and years went as such: get on medication to treat anxiety and depression (Prozac); gain 70lbs; get a psychiatrist

(Ginsberg); get off of Prozac and get newer medication with less side effects; get a therapist (Wampler); join a bi-polar support group (DBSA); learn to set boundaries; start working out again; start eating better; get a routine that works; take control of your life; be active.

Phase two had begun. Living this life I knew that medication was not an option for me to take or leave. It was something that I needed, daily and I had to simply figure what my life would look like now that I was taking medication for a mental health condition that nobody could see but was very much real. Getting the right balance of medication was not easy. I dealt with some severe side effects. Excessive weight gain was the first notable side effect. It seems trivial, but knowing that you cannot fit your clothes anymore because you are taking medication that keeps you from going crazy is a lot to carry around. The weight gain was not just ordinary happy relationship weight. I looked like a totally different person, at least 50lbs heavier, all from medication. Another side effect was an uncontrollable movement of my tongue. I would get up in the morning to go to work and all of the sudden I could not speak.

My tongue would contort and twist in my mouth. It happened in the in-patient facility during initial psychosis onset when I was 23; and I frantically called one of my church members, mumbling through contortions, asking what was happening. I thought I was demon possessed. I blamed "Satan" because church folk blame EVERYTHING on the devil, right? It was an allergic reaction and possibly deeper condition called Tardive Dsykenisia that can develop from taking mood balancing medications. For some people, the condition turns into shaking, small tremors, tongue chewing, or twitches. My church member told me to tell the nurses, and I did. A day prior I had the same tongue contorting reaction, I was so afraid, I just curled up in a ball and cried in the corner of my room at the facility, tongue contorted, sobbing and rocking. A nurse found me and asked how long I had been like that. I didn't know. I only knew that I had not done anything to deserve whatever was happening to me.

If I had asked someone else, who knows what advice they would have given me. My experience was unique to my circle. I had not heard anybody else that I knew describe what I was going through. Nobody that I knew in my family had ever taken any type of mood balancing medication. I did not know any Black people who were taking medication for anything other than diabetes, gout, or high

blood pressure. It was a heavy load to carry alone. You are doing

everything you know to do, but the weight is just too heavy. This

weight often flew in on the wings of people's opinions who were "just

trying to help." It did not help. Often times, that help and those

opinions made me feel like shit. I felt shittier than shit because it was

my fault for being in this situation. Why couldn't I just be normal? That

was a real question that came up several times. If I knew why. If I

knew how to be any other way at the time, I would have jumped at it.

But there was no quick fix, especially when I was keeping up with life

as I knew it. No pause. No additional information. Simply maintaining

the status quo.

15
MOSAIC

My Wellness Journey is more recursive than cyclical or linear because past and present connect and intersect all the time. When a person breaks down to the point where they are totally dependent on others to care for them and meet their basic needs, as I did, the ability to survive and thrive becomes a constant litmus test of wellness. I had to remind myself that progress and wellness will vary at different stages of my life. It may seem like I have declined in one or more areas of life, but the spring forward is always a huge leap beyond where I was previously. My new perspective is that during my seeming declines in any area, it was not a setback, but a set up to launch forward. When we study nature, most animals that leap far crouch down to gain momentum, strength and the gift of gravity before leaping. Even as an athlete, we often step, rock, or reach back to gain enough momentum to propel us forward. If I were shooting a jump shot, maybe I needed to correct my form a little more to support the shot better. In the triple jump, at times I needed to move my marker back a bit further to pick up more speed, jump further, and leap longer. In essence, I was too close. I needed to reach further back to take me higher, high enough to reach my destination. I also think of sinking lower to reconnect, recharge, and revive at home base: Root to rise.

The ostrich is a widely known symbol used to depict avoiding responsibility, often a visual for the phrase "burying your head in the sand." What may not be widely known is the misinterpretation of the ostrich having its head in the sand. The ostrich places its head in the sand to be closer to the earth's core, feeling the vibration, in order to ground itself in times of danger or uncertainty so that it can get a sense of direction for survival. We may also be familiar with the Energizer Bunny, famous for outlasting the Duracell battery that conveniently burns out at the height of activity without warning. Like a super nova, it dashes out the gate, robust with activity, then wanes and slows to a complete halt. Just as it is with those elements, so is it with the physical and even the metaphysical. For the physical, an important lesson was proper recharge time.

For me, it was discovering what that is. Since I tend to absorb more emotional energy, unresolved conflicts of any kind, it literally sucked the life out of me, leaving me drained in every area of life.

After a major conflict, it is necessary for me to recharge everything—

mind, body, and spirit—meaning that I need physical, spiritual and

emotional nourishment: something to eat, a place to emotionally

release, space to move, etc. These are things that I know about myself

now, including learning how to pull my energy back and direct it.

Learning to adjust what and how much I allow in and out of my inner

sphere, these are the things that took me 44 years (and counting) to

figure out.

My stay in the in-patient care facility and psychosis took my

friends, family, and me by surprise. Up until then, I never had major

surgery, other than bronchitis as a newborn. None of us thought that I

would ever come back from that decline. I had no idea what I had

done wrong. I was just living—only doing what I had always done: do

what I feel, eat what I want, fit in with the rest. I had no idea that late

hours, overexertion, processed foods, and emotional repression was

toxic for me. And yet at age 46, though I know more about myself than

I did at 23, there are still things that I am learning, not only about

myself, but about life in general and my human existence in it. There

are other facets to my being that factor in as well, that inform who I am: such as my African and Black American heritage. I am not certain

of what specific ancestral trauma has passed down to African

Americans through generations. Scientific research has taught us that

trauma travels through our DNA, even changing the way the brain is

wired: Epigenetics. The bright side is that loving interactions and

intentional wellness can help offset and repair the impact of trauma.

For me, it was imperative to learn these connections; not to dwell on

past events, but to be informed so that I can be intentional moving

forward. This doesn't mean that we are going to magically be without

illness, but it can mean that I can walk toward wellness instead of

accepting illness as my normal. Or simply dooming myself to be

miserable. After all, if I have generational trauma; I also have

generational joy, abundance and healing, as well. I notice the former

and choose to walk in the latter.

In looking over my life and even through my personal conflicts,

I have always been searching for a sense of wellness, a sense of home.

When I bounced back from my break down and started taking my

medication consistently and going to psychotherapy, I thought I was

well. And to the credit of my commitment to being well and my

therapist, Pat Wampler, Psychiatrist and doctor, I did thrive. I was a success story. The rest was just unwritten. The shame of "illness" hung

low over my head. Though I was functioning, high functioning, I did

not feel "well". I felt pieced together by the thinnest thread, but I did

not know what to do about "it". I did not know that I had a choice to

be any more well. After I got a handle on my finances and purchased

my first home, I thought I was well. I had money in the bank. I had my

own house. That had to be what wellness was, right? Though I was in

my own house and it was a major accomplishment, I was dangerously

depressed and disconnected. I was lonely in a way that was both

visible and palpable. I worked on being more social, getting out more

and dating. I got into several relationships, but I did not bring ALL of

me along. How could I explain my one week stay in a mental care

facility? Or it was the other extreme of oversharing: Him: So how have

you been? Me: Well, before we go any further, I just have to let you

know that I've been diagnosed with bi-polar disorder. Him: Oh ok, I

was really asking about how you've been these last two days...but that

works too, I guess. Enter ghosting, then gas lighting, and my own self

sabotage. Still, I thought that the life that I was living was well. I had a

job as a teacher. I was making strides and receiving accolades at work.

I was involved in church. I had a small network of friends that I interacted with and stayed in close contact with my family. I took my medication regularly. I went to bed at a reasonable enough hour for the medication to work its way through my system by the morning time. I was well. I was as well as I knew how to be at that point in my life.

We are whole people, all of us, with layers of stories and triumph, healing and struggle. It is all a part of the human experience. None of it is better or worse than anyone else's. Seriously, it's not. The only way to show up is as ourselves, however that may be. Some scholars say that this—this authenticity, this courage, confidence, and awareness to be ourselves—is the most difficult thing for us to do. It is in these moments where I gave myself room, time, and space to sit in the stillness and busyness of my mind that I was able to create that space for love and acceptance.

What does it really mean to be well? My Maci asked me this question for a school journalism project: Tami, what does it mean to be well? I tried my best to answer her. According the Substance Abuse Mental Health Service Administration (SAMHSA), wellness has eight dimensions. Using that model, this is what wellness looks like to me:

Mental Wellness. Being aware of my thoughts and thought patterns. Using mindfulness and meditation to help clear mental blockages and usher in positive, affirming energy. Sending positive thoughts and energy to myself and others. Mentally wishing myself and others well, or to process and digest heavy, complicated emotions. May we all be well is my constant intention, but I do not always have the capacity to hold space for others. And that awareness is mental wellness.

Emotional Wellness. Being able to handle the stressors of life and respond to conflict while still inwardly being at peace. Being free of overwhelming emotions that impact my ability to accept and connect with myself and others. Free from invasive, racing, and intrusive thoughts or negative self-talk. Being loving with myself first, and others next, expressing love. Using meditation and movement to release negative or excess emotions or energy and ushering in affirming, loving and accepting energy towards myself and others. Loving freely. Expressing freely. This includes purposefully directing anger, sadness, or grief. Equanimity: a calm disposition and evenness in emotions.

PhysicalWellness. Being free of excessive pain and discomfort and free from excessive fatigue. Using nutrition and movement to help support my physical health and overall wellness goals. More specifically, having enough energy and strength to physically experience and participate in life. And resting both my body and my mind. Getting good sleep, and balancing effort with ease.

Financial Wellness. Maintaining a personal budget and generating enough wealth to take care of my basic needs which allows me to do things that I enjoy without overextending myself financially. Having a financial legacy that allows for freedom. Freedom of fulfilled needs and wants and contribution to society through financial philanthropy.

Social Wellness. Building loving and sustainable relationships with my family and others that are free from excessive conflict and confusion, filled with love, joy, and lightheartedness. Purposeful and easy connections that are supportive, fun, joyful and light.

Spiritual Wellness. Connecting with and believing in a power greater than myself that ties into my existence and purpose on this Earth. Believing in the interconnectedness of all things and that the Universe does truly have my back. Connecting to the Divine essence within myself and recognizing the Divine essence in others. Knowing and acknowledging that I am a spiritual being in a physical body.

Environmental Wellness. Realizing my connection with nature and working to do my part to preserve and sustain the natural processes, working in harmony with nature.

Intellectual Wellness. Accessing skills and the ability to think clearly, complete tasks, and learn new skills that are critical to my well-being and accomplishing goals to help myself, my community, and the larger world. Tapping into and operating in my unique gifts and talents for fun, and if I choose, as a living as well.

Occupational Wellness. Using my gifts and talents to contribute to society in a meaningful way as a career, through volunteering, or in philanthropy. Being recognized and respected for my contributions in a way that aligns with my values and belief. Connecting with other colleagues in a safe and affirming way that contributes to the well-being of others and pays a living wage that allows financial freedom.

There was a time when I looked at long bouts of isolation, emotional

outbursts and ruminating on conflicts as my normal behavior. Or I

looked at floating checks or a negative bank balance as just a regular

part of my life. Having a wellness goal for these aspects of life helps

me gauge where I can coast and see where I can put in some

intentional effort for improvement or acceptance. It also gives me permission to let go of any limiting beliefs, poor habits, or negative

social patterns that I have inherited either by family dynamics, social

constructs, or my own imagination. The action of harshly judging

myself in areas where I am actually doing well and not realizing

opportunities for growth in other areas is equally damaging. This had

me placing energy and emphasis in the wrong areas; whereas, looking

at the larger picture just helps me to set my goals. If we have a

framework, a goal, and marker for wellness that we can use as a

measure or target, then we free ourselves from relying on limited,

exaggerated or skewed information that we may have received along

the way. A continuum allows us to let go of the "this is the way it has

always been done" syndrome and gives us both permission and power

to achieve ultimate wellness. And beyond. For me, my conditions were

not chronic because I did not take heed to certain "doctor's orders".

My normal way of living created a chronic condition because I did not

know that I was supposed to be living life in any other manner than

the way I was living it. Maintaining the status quo nearly destroyed

me.

We are often taught this simple strategy to living the good life:

Listen to your parents. Do well in school. Go to college. Get a good job. Meet a nice boy/girl (perhaps in college). Be a good worker. Save some money for retirement. Give back to your community. Buy a house. Have some kids (maybe 2). Get a pet. Attend church. Pay your tithes. Eat a balanced diet. Get some exercise. Live a good life. Die then go to heaven.

People do not go in-depth about the hyphen. Between Sunrise— Sunset. *The hyphen is everything in between*. It includes the decisions that are being made, the steps that need to be taken and even the structures and dynamics that take place in between "Once upon a time...The end". The Angels and The Devils are placed securely in the details. My major question became: What happens when you are not well enough to work? When either mentally, physically, or emotionally we are not able to consistently contribute to or pursue that "good job"? Our pathway to a good life looks quite different, but we are no less capable of achieving our wellness. We only need a few more tools in our toolkit that are uniquely for us. Wellness is our inheritance as human beings.

Sometimes life takes a turn and we need a recharge or reboot. I call this creating A PAUSE. Only in a perfect world can you find everything you need, have answers to all the questions and know absolutely everything. In a perfect world we are divinity personified. Some belief systems spend a lot of time discussing the divine human, which may seem like an oxymoron to many and the missing piece for others. I know this to be true within myself. My peace is strong when I feel connected on the inside, not the outside. To me, that is God.

Though I am a scholar having studied Curriculum & Instruction and published works that focus on a more responsive approach to education, specifically with culture and curriculum, I come to this subject of wellness as both a practitioner and a scholar, applying my knowledge of research and research systems to real occurrences in my life. I am the subject, participant, client, student, researcher and teacher. I draw from the greatest minds in the fields of nutritional, social, psychological and medical sciences and dare to implement their suggested best practices. After all, if we do not put the theories into practice and provided feedback, how will we ever bridge that gap between hypothesis and actionable results? And I draw on my own knowledge of research as an urban education scholar, bringing the

Afrocentric lens to the discussion of inherited trauma, toxic stress,

nutrition, finances and wealth building, emotional wellness and

mindfulness to contribute my lived and learned experiences in hopes

of adding to the conservation, broadening the perspective, and

introducing the concept of intentional holistic and integrative wellness

to a society that said "Pull yourself up by the bootstraps" then cut off

our feet and stole our boots.

16
IN PLAIN SIGHT

In the recent past, I recall seeing continuous postings of celebrities and public figures succumbing to suicide or death by lifestyle pressures. Most notable in my mind are Robin Williams, Amy Winehouse, Anthony Bourdain, and Black Lives Matter Activists MarShawn McCarrell and Edward Crawford. Historically, the life and legacy of Zora Neal Hurston, Billie Holiday, Nina Simone, and Donnie Hathaway are etched in my mind when I think of Minds as Well. I often wonder, "How differently would their legacies have lived out if we as individuals and a collective had a clearer vision of both what it means and what it takes to be well?" I think of classmates and family members that I know who died by suicide. I think of my own thoughts of suicide, ones that I have had at varying stages during my recovery, how I noticed the changes in my own mind and body; and how I felt, both fear and comfort, at how familiar it seemed death had become with me. I will say this. I have dealt with depression and anxiety, no secret there. I have felt hopeless; have been in so much emotional pain that I wanted to die, not because I didn't want to live, but because I was tired and wanted the pain to stop.

August 2018, I felt a heaviness that I never felt before. The emotional weight of despair on me was unbearable. The first thing I was prompted to do was lay down until the weight lifted. I promised myself I would, and I did. The second was to replenish my nutrients: I made a blueberry and pineapple smoothie with almond milk (both are known mood boosters and depression lifters). I now manage my life with a regimen of proper rest, nutrition, exercise and love. I recognize how important work life balance is but also realize that I need help to maintain this balance. This help goes beyond "Thinking good thoughts." Keeping these tanks full helps me stay balanced. I do my preparation in times that I feel great because I know there will come a time where I can't even get out of bed. I don't know why; it just is my reality. What I do know is that I'm determined to live the most abundant life I can. My heart goes out to anyone who has crumbled under the weight of depression for any reason. Living is hard as hell...no lie. Everyone's journey is different...but you matter and you are loved. For those who do not understand depression and suicide, it's ok to just be quiet.

Having my nervous breakdown in such a dynamic way on a large scale in the public eye at an unexpected juncture, I had so many questions about myself and my beliefs. In reality I could only take life little by little, one step at a time. I now realize that the same process for me is necessary to lean into myself: allow the pieces of me to unfold little by little whenever they are ready to unfold. I am multi-dimensional. You are multi-dimensional. We are all multi-dimensional. There is no box big enough to place me in; there is no place small enough to disappear into. In my second reflection of my life experiences, I set out to explore Happiness and I emerged with what I considered to be Five Pillars of a Happy and Fulfilled Life. This was before I discovered the Eight Dimensions of Wellness, the Eight-Fold Path, Bram viharas, Kwanzaa principles, Ikigai,

Ubuntu, Hygge, and Radical Self-Care. But you could not tell me

that I had not discovered the holy grail of pursuing happiness

and I am still going to share my insight.

Over twenty years ago, right after my nervous breakdown, I

set out to write a book about friendship: *How to be a friend and*

maintain friendships. This desire came from examining my own

friendships and seeing them change right before my eyes. For

instance, there are people that I was once enamored with and

who were enamored with me that I no longer even speak to.

There are, also, those friends that are still somewhere in my

view, but the connection is lost. They are there, but we no

longer have a speaking or even an energetic connection. Some

speak of these connections as our soul tribe. I have friends that I

speak to regularly and have worked on projects with and there

are those that I desire friendship with, but this reality seems

elusive. While in 1999 I felt as though I had all the answers, so

much that I was going to write an entire book about it, here I am

some twenty plus years later still exploring this concept,

expanding and growing. And the field of mental health is

continuing to expand, even with nutritional psychiatry and the

value of lived experiences of recovery and resilience.

I have been a part of many communities. Communing

together is a concept that was seared into me at a young age in

the most loving way. My mother—the only girl of five brothers

and middle child with two older brothers and two younger

brothers—has always been involved with her family, even when

we lived far away from Chicago and Louisiana. My father—one

of twelve siblings with six boys and six girls and a whole host of

extended family members—has always remained close with his

entire family, through family reunions and gatherings. Both sides

of my family have developed and maintained close knit family

ties all throughout with well attended family reunions and

regular family meet ups. Close ties, however, does not always

mean connection. That part, the connection piece, is inner work:

go inward to connect outward. True bonds can only be formed

and remain through a strong healthy sense of self, which

ironically happens with our own inner work merging with our outer interactions.

In adulthood, I have remained active, philanthropically, through active sorority membership, civic organizations, community advocacy and peer network facilitation. A Facebook memories post of one of Iyanla Vanzant's from 2015 appeared in my Social Media feed. Her original post read: "We must bring a strong sense of self and purpose into a relationship. We must bring a sense of value, of who we are. We must bring an excitement about ourselves. Value, purpose and vision. That's what love is about." (Iyanla Vanzant, June 8, 2015 8:30AM). My repost read: "I think we forget this and sometimes we lose sight of who we are when we get in relationships, thus losing the qualities that attracted us in the beginning. Relationships are not about changing for the other person, but about becoming more of your true self. Change is inevitable but the change must be into more of YOU and not your partner."

(June 8, 2015, T. McEwen, On This Day).

Mind as Well

I was beaming with excitement when I saw the article for the Liberate meditation app, created by a Black man for Black people. Yes! I had just gotten a contract to provide meditation and stretch classes at a local country club and needed a bit more guidance leading a full meditation class. I had only been led in meditation during yoga teacher training for maybe 30 minutes at a time or on my own through Faith Hunter's 30-Day meditation, which was 10 minutes at the most. The option to dive deeper into a meditation practice specifically for the Black Indigenous People of Color (BIPOC) community was intriguing. I downloaded the app and the first meditation was Unveiling Our Deepest Goodness, Pamela Ayotunde. I settled into my seat. I closed my eyes. I took a deep inhale through my nose then out through my mouth. I adjusted to make sure I have support for my back as she admonished. I put down anything that was in my hands, at her urging. I accepted the invitation to rest. To be still and quiet. To lean into my deepest goodness. I spent at least 30 minutes with her that day and even more time scrolling through the Liberate Meditation app. Then I saw that the Liberate community would be holding live meditation sessions in response to the pandemic and heightened racism aimed at the BIPOC community. I joined the sessions. For four months I was part of the Liberate Meditation community; looking across the screens at this beautiful sea of Black faces, all shades and associations. Then I joined the Peer Facilitators to now be one of three Meditation space holders for our Tuesday noon sits. For two months, I co-led the beautiful meditation space for the BIPOC community. I continued on teaching my meditation and stretch class at the local country club until COVID social distancing restrictions made it unsafe to do so.

This was one of the many communities I have been blessed to be a part of. I chose to end my peer meditation facilitation as I was moving more towards financially sustaining projects and away from volunteering; not because I did not want to volunteer, but because I had to be honest about my financial situation. I had been unemployed from a regular W2 earning job since February 20, 2019. It was now June 2020 and income was not flowing in, yet I was always active. I had been more active

outside of having a regular W2 that I had when I was clocking

into work daily. Only this time, I did not have the paystub to

show it. I had some huge decisions to make. Here I was, the

community advocate sitting on boards, serving on committees,

hosting wellness spaces, and I was not earning enough income

to support myself; working odd jobs at Instacart until the

Pandemic caused me to pause. I even contracted for a local

political campaign, which brought in consistent income, along

with my two months assignment as a US Census Enumerator. As

much as I loved holding space, having five people pay $10 for a

yoga session or sporadically $50 for a wellness consultation, was

not sustainable. I had a plan for a full wellness initiative and

even had a pricing structure and had applied for several grants.

Nothing sustainable was coming in. I was faced with a major

decision: Am I going to let the practice that has healed me be

the practice that kills me?

After taking a course with the Small Business Association (SBA) regarding cash flow, the presenter admonished us to not only write out our services and products, but to also look at what our life costs and determine what is needed to achieve that end figure based on what we already do or provide. This started to seem like an uphill climb since I did not have a lot of money when I started this business venture. I wanted to stay in wellness, but the business aspect of the wellness industry was taking more from me than I had to give.

For me, that excitement about myself is what I had been missing, rather what I had lost. Not in formation, but in sustainability. Emotional insecurity is a term that resonated strongly with me. Not in a sense of needing to diagnose, but as a reminder of the parts of me that often require a bit more attention and care. Emotional nurturing is the gift that I have learned to give myself, becoming more aware. Some communities I have been a part of are still intact. Others have fallen away or been completely dissolved. Regarding community,

I have had to ask myself: Who am I watering? Who is watering

me?

Regarding community I have often found my well running

dry. That must mean that I am pouring out more than I am

pouring in. There are various models of community. Thich Nhat

Hanh, Vietnamese Thien Buddhist monk, founder of the Plum

Village Tradition, shares that the Sangha is not a place to hide in

or escape to, but it is a place to be refueled and refilled, to be

replenished and revived so that we can return to our

communities and family networks to continue the wellness work

that we initially set out to do. Living yoga allows me to be the

change that I seek. It allows me to create and be a part of a

community that will continue to sustain itself. Living yoga

sustains us because it is rooted in love. Living yoga is life itself.

17
BLACK GIRL LOST AND FOUND

At forty-six years old, I have experienced enough of life to have both a comprehensive and objective view of myself. I have done a little bit of living: lived overseas, bought a house, sold a house, moved to another state, traveled and studied abroad, acquired a few degrees, done some philanthropic work, started a business, adapted a new lifestyle, embraced new philosophies of living, buried close loved ones, been "fired" from a job, quit a job, lived comfortably, lived with very little means, pursued a new career, established myself as a thought leader, had a complete halt in cash flow, experienced conflict (friends, family, co-workers, and community members), experienced physical illness, experienced mental illness, and lived to tell the story and essentially make sense of it all.

Whereas in a previous mindset I would look at these happenings as a phenomenon of some sort, I now see them as life. There are universal threads and happenings in life that I have come to know and make sense of as they arise. I have also come to see them as a part of me. All of these things are true. All of these things are me. And these things remain: Faith, Hope, Love. But the greatest of these is LOVE.

Who am I now? Who have I been? Who am I becoming? Life and all that is in it is a continuous process of becoming or unfolding into ourselves. Who I am now is a combination of who I have been and who I am becoming. I have learned and am still learning to completely embrace and accept my whole self. Many psychologists and social scientists have published their framework for stages of development. As I look over my lived experiences, this concept model is what frames my view of the stages of transformation of mindset becoming and unbecoming:

I am.

I Live.

Life happens.

Life happens to me.

Life happens because of me.

Life is influenced by me.

Life is me.

I am Life.

I am.

CENTERED

"I do love myself. I just seem to have gotten some of the dust from other's doubt and disbelief on me." I wrote these words at the top of one of my journal pages. Writing reflection has always been a way to release my emotions. I somehow walked away from what I knew to be true and attempted to walk in other people's truths, when in reality, the best thing I can do for me and others is have a life well lived on my own terms. I realize that I help others by overcoming and applying what I learn from others and telling my story. We all have a story to tell, and the truth of that story helps others to walk their paths. I met the founder of Genius is Common, and he asked me what my superpower was since everyone has one. At first I said authenticity, then I said transparency. After further thought, my superpower is that I am liberated within myself. There is nothing I will not learn, try, or implement to unshackle my own self or move towards progress. I believe in personal growth and rarely need or depend on an entourage to make it happen.

If I see something, dream something, visualize something I will walk towards it with no holds barred. This I know for certain. Master escape artist. I believe in being freed from anything that may be binding me. Like an air balloon, I'm hard to pin down. I am just now realizing that this is exactly where I'm supposed to be: Free to fly and explore whatever and wherever I desire. I do love a home base, a launch pad or Lilly pad to return to. But I am most happy being free and clear.

I accept all parts of me. I accept that I am ever evolving in word, thought, philosophy, experience and beliefs, as well as capability. I acknowledge that at times I get stuck in a certain mindset. I acknowledge that me believing that the stuck place is where I belong is what keeps me stuck. I make a true commitment to get unstuck, to move forward both figuratively and literally. I appreciate the life that I have lived and those that have crossed my path. I commit to living in my now and only in my now.

UNTANGLING THE CORDS: JUST BE.

It is important to understand that a large part of wellness involves a process I call *untangling the cords of our unconscious creation*. Because we are constantly becoming, the reality is that we created some situations in our unaware state and we may have to intentionally untangle those cords. Maybe it is the friendships that we are in, jobs we took, careers we entered, houses we built, dietary decisions we made, or the lifestyle choices that impact our health, wellness, or finances. We awake in the thick of what we created. We must take time to untangle those cords. For me, part of those cords were with my family; others were with my own choices, apart from anyone else.

We were the typical family. Taking family trips. Searching for the golden egg during Easter egg hunts in the living room. Making pallets on the living room floor and having slumber parties when our cousins came over. Sunday mornings at church and going to bed early so Santa Clause would leave a gift under the tree instead of a lump of coal in my clogs outside of the door. We laughed nonstop. When I look back at my childhood there is laughter. There is love. There is, also, the stark reality that adulthood clarity brings to childhood memories. There is the adult realism that explains why my parent's divorced and the clarity that helps me to understand just because my family unit is

not what it was when I was a child, that does not mean that I come

from a broken home. That does not mean that I am broken. Over time

I learned that I was not broken, that I could define my existence for

myself. I did not have to be victim to society's labels of what growing

up in a single-family home was or even what it meant to be a single

family. Instead of owning my experiences, I thought I had to portray

perfection. I had never learned that my only mission on this planet

was to simply be. I am enough, period. This lesson came in waves

throughout my life, but I must say that all roads lead to this truth: Just

be. Just be.

18
GOOD MORNING MOTHER AFRICA
(Through my eyes while studying abroad Summer 2010)

Gauteng—The City of Gold

She is I and I am she.

You called me daughter, stretched out your arms and said, "Welcome home."

You greeted me with your hills of gold, your rhythmic chants, and celebratory dance.

You taught me Xhosa—I responded Ngiyabonga!

You taught me Zulu—I responded, Ndiyabulela!

You showed me your battle scar of wars lost and won.

And still you danced. Still, you laughed. Still, you cried. Still, you prayed.

You lulled me to sleep with the silence of the night,

And led me to your backyard where the lions roam free.

You let me dine at your table and sleep in your beds.

You whispered, "eat now" and then said, "rest my child."

You shared with me your culture.

As I looked into your eyes, I saw the reflection of my own.

As I touched your skin, I felt the warmth of my own.

Mother Africa, thank you for letting me come home.

To you I say Ngiyabonga! and Ndiyabulela!

PART FOUR

BEYOND

19

LIBERATION

I saw fear clearly.
Stood trembling and feebly.
Staggered to the edge of destiny,
Then shrank underneath lies and deceit.
She adorned herself in falsehood and confusion
Kept calamity and deception close by
While faith hung in the balance, muffled.
I see fear clearly.
Black heart scorned with memories of failure.
Eyes wide shut with mouth open and heart closed.
Then stillness breezes by with the sweet
Fragrance of hope on the wings of love.
Faith embraces fear with gentle caresses of
Purpose and Reassurance.
Whispering affirmations.
One step.
Joy celebrates the small victories.
Another step.
Purpose gently pushes forward.
Motion.
Love activates Action.
Faith follows; Fear fades.
Liberation.

20
LIVING YOGA

What does the practice of yoga look like for a person like me? My reality is that I am a combination of many things, people, cultures, and experiences. I connect by finding the truth in every experience and making it my own; that is the only way that I know how to do it. This process requires knowing myself and sitting with myself long enough to know what fits and what does not, but remaining open and flexible enough to learn from that which does not fit. There is a belief in yoga that nothing is lost on this journey. This aligns with a Christian principal that I grew up believing: *All things work together for the good of those that love the Lord and are called according to His purpose.* These are concepts learned during my yoga training that brought comfort and ease to my journey through this life. Some of the principles reminded me of lessons and philosophies I had known all my life:

We are all connected.

All living things are connected by a central and Universal thread that transcends race, gender, culture, and economic status. Returning to the centrality of our humanity is the bond that connects us all. We are

all connected.

Our existence is made up of our interaction with ourselves, our

interaction with others, and interactions with the larger society. How

we interact with ourselves frames how we interact with others and

how we show up in the world. At times, the flow shifts: our

relationship with others influences our relationship with ourselves,

and this frames how we interact with the larger society. At other

times, societal occurrences impact us so greatly that we reflect on our

relationship with ourselves, or others, and that influences all factors:

how we interact with ourselves, how we interact with others, how we

show up in the world.

We belong to no one and no one belongs to us. We are in an

equitable relationship with all living beings that requires mutual

respect, understanding of purpose, an ebb and flow or Ying and Yang.

Our interaction with other living beings is a constant awareness: giving,

receiving, and letting go. If our voice is too loud, we will drown out

necessary instruction. If our voice is too soft, a necessary message of

ours will not be heard. Liberation is our birthright as living beings.

Impermanence is the understanding that nothing lasts forever just as it is. We are always adjusting or in motion, yet finding stillness is our peace. Motion does not have to mean overextension. There is a stream in motion that allows us to coast and catch our breath or recharge and rest in the stream of work that has been done. Knowing when to pump, coast, glide, and glean is our individual lesson. It is the wisdom of our lived experiences that helps to light our path forward. The body, the mind, the breath, all work in tandem to bring ease of well-being. Sitting with myself and seeing the many ways that I am an individual, yet, interconnected allowed me to reflect and return to this principle of living as needed. We are not given a fixed set of prescribed instructions, but principles and guidelines to apply to our situation so that we are empowered at each level.

Meditation, Movement, Pranayama, Meals: We create space for our emotions through meditation and stillness. Allowing time for reflection, breath, and noticing allows a natural inner settling and cleansing to occur. There is nothing to fear in this process. It helps to move forward mindfully and be more aligned as we move through life.

The more flexible and focused we are, the more we can grow and expand. What we resist persists and there is no fast track or rapid release for inner growth. When things are stalled and completely out of our control, we rest in the comfort of surrender. We can see ourselves as accepting or rejecting ideals and experiences based on how well they align with where we are, skills we have, and what we are seeking to accomplish or understand.

I turn to the principles of grammar and function of parts of speech in examining progress in our lives: action and being. Verbs, which represent movement, demonstrate two main states: action or being. Action verbs show tangible movement, but states of being demonstrate existence; both are equally important. In making progress sometimes we must physically move our body through *asana,* (yoga positions or poses) and mindful movement. Other times progress is made through shifting or expanding our perception through our state of mind: "as a man thinks in his heart so is he." In living yoga principles, start with the practical and move to the spiritual as it makes sense to you and you can understand. The Eightfold Path of Yoga brings union: Mind & Body balance for functioning and connection with Spirit. My practice begins and ends with a deeper look into me: how I relate to myself, how I relate to others, how I

make sense of and show up in the world.

21

FLESH, BONE, AND BEYOND

We are more than just flesh and bone. This concept is explored deeply in any spiritual text and goes beyond a religious doctrine to the core of our human existence. This is explored in Yoga Philosophy through the Koshas also known as the Five Layers of Ourselves or our five bodies. Interesting enough, I had studied each one of these concepts of self in some form throughout my lifetime: formally and informally in my own pursuit. Yoga's model of self with the *Koshas* is my first conscious look at how all of these parts of the self exist in all of us and can work together for us or against us. The practice of awareness helps to bring our attention back to what could be at the root until we accept that we just are: I am=Atman or Soul

Here are our five layers, or the "Layers of the Self" also known as the Koshas explained. It is the many layers of who we are, our many selves that all require attention, nurturing and care. These are essential components of who we are as human beings. We see the physical layer, but we are far more than flesh and bone. I often say that as humans we are multi-dimensional but often have a one-

dimensional view of each other or interact in a one-dimensional way.

The Koshas remind me that there are many layers to each person,

including myself:

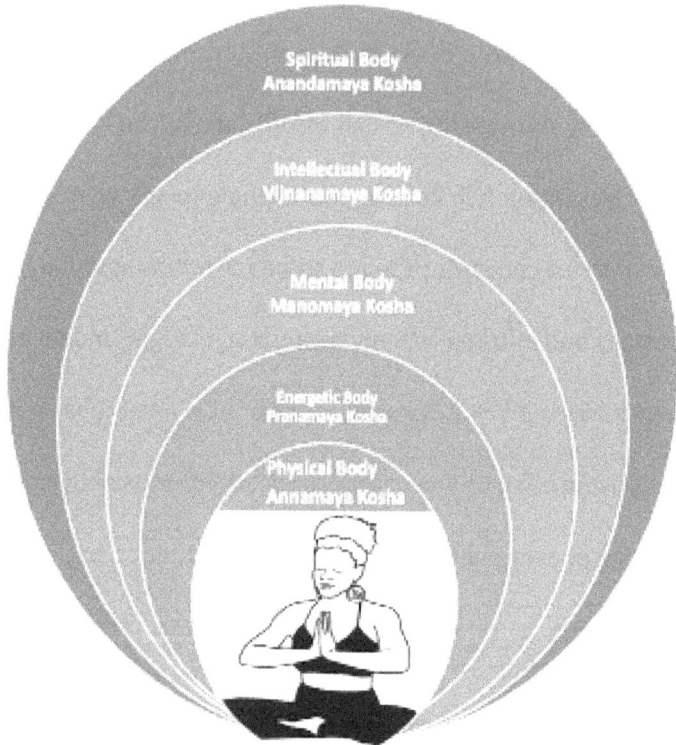

Physical: (*Annamaya Kosha*) Physical body consists of our organs,

bones, muscle, tissues, and skin.

Anna = Food or Physical

Maya = Made of

Ayurveda, the nutritional science and sister practice to yoga can help to align food and nutrient intake for a well body. It takes into consideration mind types and body types in three categories: *Vata, Pitta, Kapha* mind and body types. These foods each align with natural elements and can impact our minds and our bodies in various ways: such as being or feeling light, heavy, racing, fiery, cool, calm, bitter, or sweet. Earth, Wind, Fire, Water, Ether are the elements that come to mind. Both our bodies and our minds can represent those qualities. Foods can be a tool for balance. According to Ayurveda, our physical selves have three states: Balanced, Deficient, Excessive. We really are what we eat.

I took my first Dosha test during yoga teacher training. Before then, I had never even heard of a Dosha. My mind body type then: Vata Body, Vata Mind. In short, Vata body is a slender, rather willowy physique. Vata mind is one that envisions and imagines greatly, a creative, fantastical thinker with a mind that is spiritually connected and sensitive to subtleties in human interaction. A vata mind benefits from space to create with a routine to practically complete the many projects that a vata mind typically engages in. When balanced, a vata mind is creative, intuitive, spiritually aware, and free. When unbalanced, a vata mind can be manic, disoriented, critical, indecisive, co-dependent, and non-committal. The vata body when balanced is lean, swift, flowy, and flexible. When unbalanced, the vata body is underweight, fatigue, dehydrated, run down, and rigid. When I came to the practice of yoga, I was dealing with the physical manifestation of illness in my body by way of uterine fibroid tumors, stiffness and pain in my wrists and fingers upon waking up, and breakouts through my skin. I learned that the food I consume can have a direct impact on my physical body. I began to become more mindful of eating for wellness in a more systematic way, with awareness, so that my physical body could be well. A practical application of this philosophy is to eat the colors of the rainbow with a variety of flavors, textures and temperatures. Eating mindfully is fully taking in the smell, taste, and texture of food; taking time to enjoy and fully engage in our meals without multitasking; giving thanks and honoring our food source, even pondering the process of food harvesting. These are examples of eating mindfully that help our food to digest properly. Lastly, eating real food that is not chemically processed or manufactured is critical to my entire well-being. I learned the necessity of keeping food as close to the original state as possible with minimal manipulation to get the fullest life benefit for my physical body to repair itself. To preserve life, we must consume food for life, which is natural plant based non-chemically processed food.

Physiological: (*Pranamaya Kosha*) Our Physiological or Energetic body consists of atoms, cells, organs, body systems. Our energy is visible in this layer of self. Yogic breathing or Pranayama exercises, also called breathwork, directly impacts this layer of self. Our breath is the central life force and representation of life force in our bodies. The vitality and qualities of our life can be seen in our breath.

Prana = Subtle life force or Chi (Traditional Chinese Medicine)

Pumping of heart = Elimination of Waste

Subtle energy influences our state of the mind, which is the next layer of self. Yogic breathing increases and regulates prana in the body. The practice of Qigong was a reinforcement of Breath and Energy Work for me. No matter what anyone teaches, yoga begins and ends with the breath. In the practice of yoga, the breath is always present as the guiding force and key component. When we tap into our breath and let breath be our guiding and aligning force, we are soon to tap into mind body balance. This may be a lifelong practice.

Mental Body: (*Manomaya Kosha*) Our mental body consists of our mind, emotions, and nervous system. This is our streams of thought, feelings, and sensations, which make up our perceptions.

Manas = mind or thought process

Recovery of stress and fatigue is directly impacted by this layer of self. When we have a mental body that is intact and well, we are able to quickly recover from stress and fatigue. When our mental body is compromised, our ability to recover, or our rate of recovery from stress and fatigue, is directly impacted. This layer of self houses our five senses and automatic responses. It is where we receive, absorb, and process input from the world.

Ideas = Brain   Thoughts = Mind

Since our mental state frames our perception of the world and ourselves in it, our state of balance or imbalance can essentially be "hiding in plain sight".

Wisdom Body: (*Vijnanamaya Kosha*) Our intellectual layer, is the seat of our intuition, conscience, and reflection.

Vijnana = Intellect   Brain = action or state of being

Awareness of who we are and how we relate to the world around us frames the ideas we form and the actions we take. Whereas, our Mental Body is impacted by "Input", our Intellectual or the Wisdom Body is reflected in our "Output". Our input is what comes into our minds. Our output is what we mentally express. Some might even call out output our mindset: That which we have allowed to set our minds. Our wisdom body is all about action, or in some cases inaction. If we are wanting to examine our actions or inability to take action, we must turn our attention to our mental body and ask ourselves: what have we been taking into our mental body? What are we absorbing? Then do the work to purify and move beyond any limiting beliefs or "samskaras" regarding our own abilities. We are admonished to pay attention to internal sensations and pulsations for this layer of self. A regular yoga practice quiets the mental body and mind so the wisdom body can be heard.

Bliss Body: (*Anandamaya Kosha*) The Bliss or "Spiritual" layer is the state of freedom, expanse, joyousness of your true nature. It is who we are without trying to be who we think we should be. It is our true and authentic self. This is our highest self or spirit. It is who I envision myself as, living in a state of healing. It is not perfection, but rather a gateway of freedom of expression to operate within my highest intentions and highest good; this leads to ultimate union: Samadhi.

The center of the Koshas is the Self which is Atman (Soul) or Samadhi, our highest self. The highest Self is always there, never experiencing a separation from reality. Others have called the Self God, the soul, Atman, life itself, or oneness. Altogether, this is yoga. This is union: a state in which all things are connected and work together to reveal and bring about our highest good. This is a state that may very well take a lifetime to achieve. This is life. This is living yoga.

Digital Image Courtesy of Be Well, Friends LLC & Tamia A. McEwen, PhD (2019). Image may not be use without permission from Tamia A. McEwen, PhD.

So, who am I? I am body. I am breath. I am mind. I am wisdom. I am spirit. I am my awareness. I am what sense I make of the world. I am perceptions. I am curiosities. I am reflections. I am.

In taking this deep dive into who I truly am, it led to who I was before this exploration of self-began. You see, my current existence was built from my past perceptions. That meant that my current surrounding after my deep dive conflicted with my understanding of myself. I had operated unconsciously and made agreements and was now in what some would consider a Karmic reality. It was a bit of Cognitive Dissonance. I call this awareness Shadow and Light. The process, I call Untangling the Chords.

Karma is a Hindu or Buddhist concept, which is defined as "the sums of a person's actions in this and previous states of existence, viewed as deciding their fate in future existences". I am not a Buddhist, but I certainly resonate with the guidance as it relates to liberation from suffering and the causes of suffering. If there was ever a mark that I believe the Christian church missed, it is with the full service to mankind's liberation from suffering. It is with kindness and caring; it is with the fullness of love outside of doctrine or protocol; perhaps it is how we interpreted and carried out those sacred scriptures and missed doing our own inner work where the opportunities were missed. There is always time to reckon. Some individuals and fellowships have done this reckoning on their own. For that I am thankful.

22

LIFESTYLE AS WELLNESS

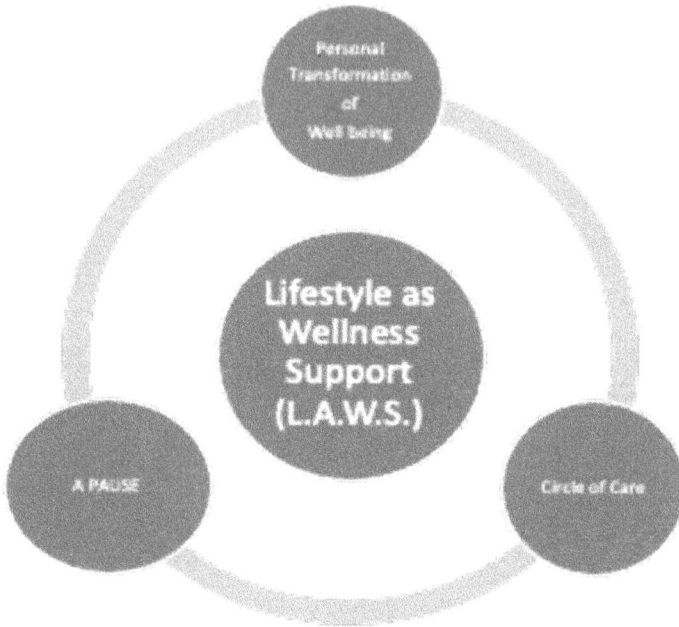

A research study conducted in the UK showed the nearly 53%

of lives are lost each year, approximately 31 million, due to

preventable lifestyle related illnesses. Along with these factors 47% of

people will experience a mental illness or mental health crisis at least

once in their lifetime. A University of Illinois study showed that of the

47% who will experience a mental health crisis, only 50% of those with symptoms with seek treatment from a medical or mental health professional.

The British Journal of Psychiatry reported that the highest impact on health and wellness is lifestyle. The greatest measure of sustainability in lifestyle change is individuality affirming the finding that 53% of debilitating illnesses are preventable through lifestyle change.

My model of Lifestyle as Wellness emerges from my own search of support measure for wellness. For me, these next components helped to remove the roadblocks to whole health and wellness and allowed me to have accessible and sustainable wellness support.

TRANSFORMATION OF WELL BEING

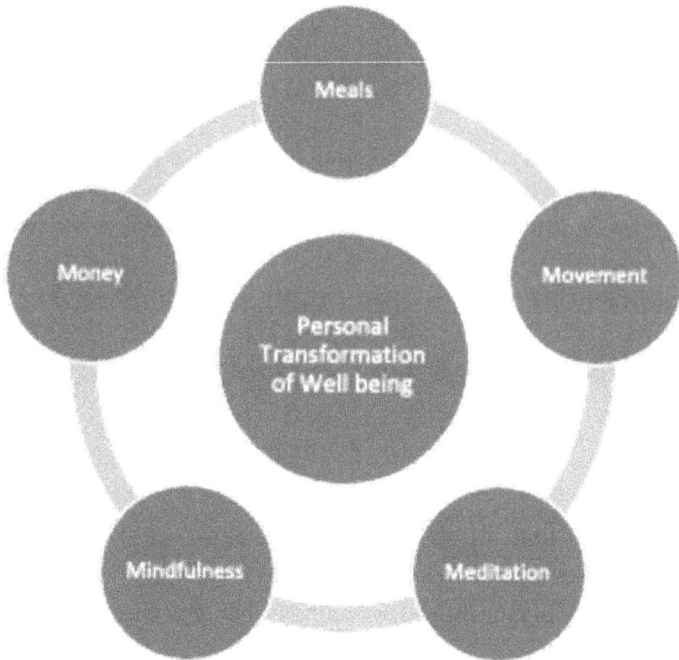

We are uniquely created and beautifully designed. I remember growing up watching Sesame Street or maybe it was the Electric Company. But the scene began with a full screen of kids engaged in some activity, then the scene would zoom out into a multi-square grid showing video panes of various kids doing an activity, and the song would begin "One of these kids is not like the other..." Of course, there might be three hula hoopers and one jump roper, and I'd look and point to identify the "odd ball". What I've come to learn in life is simply that we are unique with individual talents, yes but also individual functioning, dietary and lifestyle needs.

There is no one size fits all for wellness because what is well for one could be torture for another. Knowing what works for us as individuals and focusing on that alone without proselytizing our wellness regime and forcing it on others is important. I joke all the time that I am not the one at the barbecue knocking plates out of people's hands, kicking over grills and slapping away chicken legs. I also say, "If you see me in these streets with a rib, mind your business!" I say it jokingly—but seriously—because guilt and shame have no place in a wellness journey. In fact, it is undoing the impact of guilt and shame that usually is the work of wellness.

We all have a choice. I am not better or worse because I drink carrot juice over soda. The question is what is our goal? There are certain steps that can bring us closer to that goal and steps that move us further away, but the focus really does need to be on ourselves, of course unless we are invited elsewhere. Secondly, new information is discovered all the time about the impact something has on our system, or the way the earth's soil is producing more or less of certain nutrients and minerals. This is where being locked into nature and being restoration-minded comes in. If our goal is to restore and respect the natural process of things, we are clinging to simplicity, not loading our lives, bodies, and food with more "things". Food is neither good nor bad. The question remains, "Is it nutritious?"

Our taste buds are our taste buds. We each have an affinity for a certain flavor palette, texture, appearance, or smell of food, and that is natural. Some of us are more heightened than others with a deeper connection between our emotions and GI tract, and that is normal. Appealing food is necessary in proper digestion. We first encounter food with our smell, touch and sight before taste. The digestive process is already beginning. We want to be excited, salivating before actually tasting our food. It helps digestion. Moving forward with that in mind, the goal then is to find nutritious foods, substances, and activities that appeal to us. None of us have to suffer through for wellness, unless of course, we are moved and motivated by grueling challenges. For those who are more prone to the Zen side of things, there are plenty pathways of wellness to choose from. For every taste and texture there is a pleasing, nutritious item just waiting for us to consume it. I learned to not give up on wellness because I do not like Brussel sprouts (I love Brussel sprouts, by the

way...sauerkraut, not so much!). The question becomes: What are my

choices? Knowing there are wellness choices that can work for our

ability, budget, preference and comfort level keeps us open to

progress and forward movement.

Meditation

My first full experience with meditation was during my 200-

hour yoga teacher training; sitting crossed legged, fully upright on my

sit bones with meditation pillow beneath me. I was slightly elevated so

my knees touched the surface. I pretended to close my eyes, stealing

glimpses around the room at different intervals to see who was really

sitting with their eyes closed and participating. I believed that

meditation only required silence and stillness. But the mind as well?

How then do we quiet the mind? With my history and experience with

a mind under siege, I knew the agony of a terribly busy mind and the

distress that comes with insomnia or feeling out of sorts, disconnected

from your mind and body. The medical term is disassociation. The

actual meaning of Yoga is "to yoke." Yoga means union: union between mind and body. It is the practice of bringing all of ourselves together, harnessing our physical, mental, emotional, ethereal, energetic, and bliss bodies together in one unified vessel to ease suffering.

I grounded my personal meditation practice by following Faith Hunter's 30-Day Meditation Challenge. The practice of meditating daily, consistently for as little as 10 minutes a day was not only empowering, it was enlightening. Meditation seems so simple, but it was where I most of my internal criticism rose up. Another place where an onslaught of internal criticism arose is when I was practicing the physical asanas in yoga. The critical mind will show up, as it did in me. Without space to sit with the judgement, criticism, or whatever emotions bubble up, those emotions will not only grow, they will consume, envelope and suffocate you. The weight of the negative emotions within our own mind and body is what can and will take us under if we do not have a safe space to sit with these strong emotions; or at times release them all together. The practice of guided meditation allowed me the space to check in with myself. This provided the tools to Respond versus React to my environment. A healthy meditation practice can quickly disarm the need to "Give what we get" that sits at the root and foundation of violence, including violent conversation.

Money

My first direct experience with money management would have to be taking Dave Ramsey's Financial Peace course while I prepared to buy my first home. It was the first time I took a deep look at how money works, budgeting, saving and investing. The purpose, however, was to improve my credit enough to purchase a house and to impress my church congregation.

I know. Who achieves a 720-credit score just to impress a non-denominational, yet charismatic church group? *Me!* I was in my late twenties at the time, but I now realize at 46 years old that I was then, and still am now, quite extrinsically motivated and people driven. I live for praise, recognition, adoration, and acclaim. Being seen as responsible and accomplished had great merit and significance to me. My pastor announced the progress of young people and couples, and I wanted that recognition, too. I diligently worked to pay off debt, collections claims, overdue bills, and began to follow Dave Ramsey Financial Literacy principles of cash flow management.

I used Dave Ramsey's envelope system of separating my cash into envelopes and sticking with it. It worked. I raised my credit score, secured a mortgage loan and bought my first house at 29-years old. I built it from a concrete slab, choosing brick and grout color, roof shingles, wall paint, tile size and color, and even beveled versus standard counter-top edges. This was in the year 2003. I lived in that house for eleven years, selling it in 2014 when I moved to Florida to help be a caretaker for my grandparents, to flee a crumbling relationship, and to navigate recent conflicts in my career as a classroom teacher and leader.

As noble as I wanted my move to Florida to appear to be, Florida was my escape plan. I was able to help provide amazing care for my grandparents for their end of life, the best 9 and 13 months of my life. I grew emotionally, but also suffered a great financial blow: 35K pay cut, major career transition, complete dissolution of my IRA, new wellness business as certified yoga teacher, and the economic stalemate of a global pandemic. The good part is that I had 80K in retirement savings as a cushion and principles of financial management to lean on; but I had both a cash flow and self-worth issue that was near fatal for my budding business and finances. The correlation to self-worth and revenue as a business owner needs deep

exploration and attention. Deepak Choprah's 21 Day Abundance

Meditation took me through mantras and affirmations: *money is*

energy. That was a new concept for me, money is energy. I joined a

Black Entrepreneur Institute (BEI). I applied for and received several

gig work and independent contract level jobs. While I was away from

the career I chose—had become a scholar, PhD or "hooded" as it is

called when you receive your doctorate degree, the world changed.

And then the world turned upside down, including how the world

made or generated income to make a living.

As I write this portion of this manuscript, we have surpassed

12 months of this global pandemic—2020: The Year that Never Was.

So much has happened in the year 2020, yet it oddly feels like just

yesterday it was 2019. In reality, a whole year has passed. Some say

that blur is the presence of trauma. Some say it is avoidance and

denial. I do agree with those descriptions. I also call it life. The

haziness of life. In a pandemic I filed for unemployment for the first

time and began to think about how I generate income. The Japanese

concept of Ikigai resurfaced: What do I love? What am I good at

doing? What does the world need? In what conditions can I thrive? I began to do things I loved: volunteering in the community through legislation information, service in sewing pillow-case dresses, US Census taking, Peer Coalition Boards, Mental Health and Wellness Panels. I loved that type of work.

I had to know how much my life cost. I took to my spreadsheet in generating my projected income needs, cashflow, financial responsibilities. Financial pillars of wellness required a realistic look at the cost of my needs, wants, and responsibilities. The cost of wellness also rises significantly with risky behavior and stress inducing situations. A life committed to peace and wellness gets a greater return on the investment because a healthy mind and body is our most valuable asset. This means that how I generate income, in what conditions, is just as important as how much income I generate: a million-dollar salary with 3 million dollars' worth of stress is a liability and bankruptcy roadmap. But $75K salary and heart full of peace brings residual wealth.

Movement

The physical asanas of the yoga practice transformed my body quickly because my training was intensive: 16 days of 10-hour sessions, with at least 5 hours of physical practice daily. Within those 16 days I saw my physical body transform. I did experience some tenderness, though. I had tenderness in my wrists and also the tops of my feet. I learned over time to adjust my body alignment, taking pressure off my wrists and using a pillow or blanket to cushion the thin skin on the tops of my feet. My body, though, after 16 days, felt stronger than ever.

The concept of embodied experiences tells us that our physical bodies absorb everything that has occurred, whether energetically or physically. When we have a physical response to any situation, it is considered somatic, indicating embodiment. Embodiment means felt or experienced in the body. Movement helps energy travel throughout our body so our body can heal. We use the body to heal the body, even when we are not conscious of what is occurring. Asanas allow for the processes of energy movement, healing and alignment to happen without conscious articulation. Bessel van der Kolk reminds us that "The body keeps the score of our traumatic occurrences." As I am reading through Dr. Joy De Gruy's

Post Traumatic Slave Syndrome, and reading articles relating to epigenetics, I resonate with trauma and healing being embodied principles. Movement is medicine. Gentle movement that is calming, is medicine.

As I frantically searched for a yoga studio near me to get my personal practice back on track, I found myself locked out, but able to see the feet and ankles of all other patrons who had arrived on time. I needed a release and just could not get on my mat without being overcritical of myself. This day, I needed to be guided by someone else. I was too late and could not enter because of the lock door policy the studio had. This was at least one year prior to the Global Pandemic. Studios were full of paying yogis. I ended up, instead, at the local recreation center in a Qigong class. I was vaguely familiar with qigong from my Hope Beyond Fibroids fitness recommendations. A Black man, apparently the best in Vero Beach, led the class. John, the Cloudwalker, soon after became my Qigong instructor and embodiment guide. Mark Whitwell, the heart of Yoga, and my mentor Denise Alston, were staples in getting my personal yoga practice flowing again.

I have always been an active person, even as a child, I was always in motion. Somehow, as I grew older, I believed that movement was for children or young people. That is not the case. I do not have to be an athlete or engage in competition to move my body. Movement of any kind that feels good, provokes emotional release, calm, focus, and concentration is great for my body and for my mind; especially as a person with mood balance struggles. Mindful movement is a term that is widely used today. It allows me to examine the relationship with my body, for myself, not for anyone else. Adrenaline production and stimulating movement to release feel good hormones and clear toxins is always a plus. But moving in my body for my own self is enough. This freedom of movement also allows me to explore all of what my body can do. I took a Rocket Yoga class and did a headstand for the first time at 46 years old. Just the other day, I did a cartwheel. These combined practices of loving, mindful movement are not just healing, but enjoyable.

Meals

My meals consist of all things plant based. Living the Standard American Lifestyle (SAL), and eating the Standard American Diet (SAD) brought me dis-eases, but not anymore. For me wellness is "More than just a SALAD". As I sat in the gynecologists' office on the cold, white examination table, with my feet propped up, each one in the cold, metal stirrups, I heard the doctor cavalierly say, "Oh yeah, you got some junk in there. Best bet is to just have the hysterectomy."

Removing his gloves and motioning for me to sit up, he continued, "Yeah if you were maybe in your twenties or early thirties, I'd recommend maybe having the fibroids removed...but since you are," he glanced down at his clipboard to check my age "...42? I say just have the hysterectomy and be done with it." I was stunned. Be done with it. Done with what? My femininity? My chance of naturally giving birth? It was such a huge and permanent decision and here was this doctor talking as though he could just yank out my uterus and toss it over his shoulders with the others. I did not want that for my future, not if I possibly had other options. It was my decision alone to make. I needed to think.

I had been on the fibroid hunt for years. Many women in my close circle had their own fibroids story, many with having hysterectomies or some type of surgical removal. I had never heard of a possible natural option. I was already not a fan of surgery unless it

was absolutely necessary. My dear friend recommended I look up Chef

Ahki and Coach Gessie, Hope Beyond Fibroids Elimination Program

and the Detox Now. I read up on uterine fibroid tumors and found that

meat and dairy were main contributors of the estrogen dominance

leading to fibroids as well as obesity and stress. I began to transition

away from meat and dairy on my own, and lost about twenty pounds

in the process. I was moving in the right direction, but my periods

were still in the hemorrhaging zone every month, for six days straight.

I bled through everything and was a prisoner in my own body. I was

using the diva cup, and an overnight maxi pad still having to change

both every 30 minutes to an hour. Other times I used a super

absorbency tampon and an overnight pad together and still had to

change every 30 minutes to an hour. Other teachers and co-workers

graciously, but nervously, tapped me on the shoulder many times, "Dr.

McEwen, you have something on you." Each time, I embarrassingly

knew what that something was: blood. I felt like I was going through

some kind of twisted adult puberty, the one where I did not know my

body anymore. My period always came, I just never knew how

forceful. I was in period prison.

The onset of menstrual psychosis with paranoia, mania, and severe depression was also getting worse. Every month, like clockwork I felt everyone hated me. I was worthless. I had no value. It would be better if I just died. This caused so much tension in my relationships because I was also paranoid, sensitive to criticism and skeptical of others.

"Why do you hate me!" I'd scream at my mother, bursting into tears. "Tamia, I just don't know how to take you." My mom would share. She was just as confused about my own emotions as I. Then, like magic after about the fourth day of my menses, paranoia would begin to ease. By day six or seven, emotional levels were back down to manageable, as though nothing had ever happened. This was an emotional rollercoaster that neither me, nor anyone in my circle would survive. By January 2018, I had completely transitioned to a plant-based eating lifestyle and in summer began my yoga teacher training for stress management. My full transition began with a food list of anti-inflammatory foods, a reading of the book *The Fibroid Elimination Bible,* and a 14-day liquid detox, to flush out toxins and give my digestive system a rest. I had successfully read and completed the *10-day Green Smoothie Cleanse* written by JJ Smith and had a little knowledge about the impact of fats, salt, sugar, soda, and other

processed food on my weight from reading 6 Ways to Lose Belly Fat

Without Exercise and *Lose Weight Without Dieting or Working Out*

also by JJ Smith; but the full understanding of the connection between

nutrition and my mental, emotional and physical well-being did not

come full circle until I began the Detox Program. Self-study, and

tailoring this program to my life, was critical for me to have any

progress, especially as a person with a mental health condition.

Barreling through my own inner criticism to be open and join a group

of healing women required a lot of emotional navigation. I also

learned that wellness is not a program that can be packaged. The laws

of nature do not change. Having coaches and guides can help us to

discover what has been right before our eyes all along. My only goal is

to master my own mind, and tell the story to whoever wants to listen,

so they can master their own minds as well.

The *British Journal of Psychiatry* recommends a whole food

plant-based anti-inflammatory, gut healing meal plan as mental health

and psychosis treatment, no exceptions. I read this article after

starting the plant-based journey, having been off mood balancing

medication for almost a year, and noticing mental clarity and calm that

I never thought was attainable. I also have to note, that my entire environment was intentionally well-being centered. Living alone, I did not have to divide my time or attention between other people and things. But this also meant that if I did not cook, I did not eat. I laid on the cold floor of the bathroom many late nights and early mornings, either from a deep depression or in full manic disorientation, trying to get myself together so I could move forward. Stocking my cupboards and refrigerator with the food and materials I need; even freezing meals and smoothies is part of my routine now.

My mind needs nutrients to produce dopamine, serotonin and other mood balancing hormones to be able to function. I learned, and am still learning, how a healthy body leads to a healthy mind and vice versa. Nutritious meals are for mental health, which includes physical health. Even if I was still taking medication, or for some reason must go back to taking medication, nutrition is a staple in my lifestyle support. It begins with eating real food and steering away from processed meals. Our Standard American lifestyle and diet do not make it easy to be well. Oftentimes, in my pursuit I feel as though I am fighting the system to get nutritious food. I have been able to sustain my plant-based lifestyle, but it required me to do my entire life differently, eating and living for wellness. I now see my entire lifestyle

as wellness support.

PART FIVE

MIND AS WELL

23
THIS PEACE OF MINE

This peace of mine does not wash off like cheap lotion.

It does not blow away with the first gust of life's heavy

winds

It soothes the soul like a balm and spreads into every

crevice,

Perfectly coating the parts of me that cry out for attention.

The ashy parts.

The parts that have been dried out and crusted over

By extracting too much and replenishing too little.

The parts of me that have deep groves from rivers of tears

shed.

The parts of me that laid untouched by confusion and

disconnectedness.

This peace of mine is the balm from Gilead that my elders

sing about.

It is the Rocka' my Soul in Abraham's Bosom.

It is the Shanti, Shanti Om of the Tibetan Buddhists.

It is the cool drink of water before my soul dies.

It is the moan of wailing women.

It is the silent hum of release.

It is the laughter of babies.

Yes.

This peace of mind is here to stay.

MAKING PEACE WITH MY MIND

When out of the ordinary occurrences happen, it is easy to think, "There is something wrong with me"; especially if these occurrences do not seem to be happening with other people. Over time, after seeking ways to increase my well-being, I came to understand that wellness requires self-exploration and self-acceptance, just as I am. I like to think of my wellness journey as a continuous agreement with myself. A part of this agreement is the commitment to peace: Be in peace. Stay in peace. Surround myself with peace. This seems like a simple concept because it seems to me like there has been so much that occurred in my life that was out of my control. As I continued to learn more about myself, this world that I am in, and all the other living beings who share this space, our planet, I have come to realize that there is much that I do control, and that begins and ends with my own peace. On this journey, life begins and things happen; then we begin to influence life by our decisions, then we live the life we created; then an encounter happens—whether internal or external— and we shift; who we were is no more and we become a new person, sometimes inside, sometimes outside, sometimes both. We may become consumed with our ability to reinvent ourselves and believe

that we have control, and life continues to just happen, teaching us.

Then, we realize that life just is Life.

CORONA REFLECTIONS: THREADING THE NEEDLE ALL THE WAY THROUGH

Something old, Something new

Something broken, Something borrowed

Something repaired something blue

I often wonder just what to do

With all of these discarded pieces that may just need some glue.

Or perhaps they need a match like my favorite pair of socks

That once were two but now the other I haven't got.

Or my favorite earrings with all of the Adinkra symbols

I wore them boldly and proud.

Until I looked and was only wearing one,

The other could not be found.

I was overcome with grief. I mean I looked everywhere

Only to see it months later ground up in pieces underneath my driver's chair.

The iPad I adored, after 4 years fell on its face. Crack!

I lost my creative luster for a moment. It took almost two years to get it back.

On the issues of things broken, things borrowed, repaired or blue

Of the things that are old and of those that are new.

New and shiny is fresh, feels so good on our skin.

But new only last for a moment, until the wears of life set in.

Borrowed has a certain flavor, special sentiments sometimes.

But borrowed things go back to the owner

bringing joy— but it's theirs, not mine.

Old things carry wisdom and stories of all that they've endured.

And still show their regal value,

existing longer than some thought they should.

Blue sometimes represents sadness, but I equate blue to the sea.
Carrying the emotions of life that are sure to come to you and me.

That leaves us with the last quality, that was not originally there

And that is of those things that are in need of or have been repaired.

Every broken bone is not useless, every cracked pot is not done.

Every shattered mirror is not bad luck nor is every lost victory a bad run.

The blessing of being broken is the awareness it can bring.

Awareness that life is sometimes simply filled with a multitude of things.

Things that come and things that go. Things that we create and things we do not own.

In our times of uncertainty, we can remember this one truth:

Sometimes the difference between lost and won is simply threading the needle all the way through.

Written by Tamia A. McEwen, July 7, 2020 Corona Reflections Blog, published www.MacBeWell.com

The many edged-sword of penning a mental wellness journey is being the right kind of crazy; crazy enough to be believable, but not so crazy that you scare people away and set off alarms that you are either still in crisis or beyond salvageable and marked as damaged goods. Another is telling your story in love without telling someone else's story, one that they may not be ready, if ever, to tell. The first was painfully aware to me when after my Breakfast Club appearance in December 2019, comments noted me as a paid actress, "bat shit" crazy, tripping on some hallucinogenic, or a charlatan for views and likes. None of these are true. Other comments of hope, resilience, identification, thanks, gratitude, and praise of bravery were also in the queue. The truth sits somewhere in between. I am not a paid actor, never have been. I am also not a martyr or attention seeker or even a guru, as some people have called me. I am simply a Black woman having made sense of some of my life's occurrences, one who is still making sense of others. I am just a person who learned to see my mind as well, in whatever state it is in. I am one who sees any condition—mental health or otherwise—as a response to my environment, not a measure of weakness, but rather a reflection of humanity.

There is a double standard that applies in the behavioral health field with support and assistance. If I show up in too much of a crisis I could be admitted against my will. If I show up appearing too well put together, no one will believe I need support, and I will instead end up helping them carry their emotional load. I often found myself asking, "Where can I really go to get the help that I need?" Where can I go to have my cup filled and not have to hold space for everyone while it is being filled; or feel guilty for asking to just "sit in the pews," instead of being asked to stand in the pulpit? I must also take responsibility for my own participation in offering myself to others without them asking, or saying yes to requests although I had nothing to give. This is the gift that peer spaces, peer networks, and peer models have given me in allowing me to live out a well-being centered life; knowing that it is not selfish but self-preserving and selfless to do so. This is a lesson of boundary setting, capacity checking, and self-care that I keep on repeat. I thought I had the answer 20 years ago. Then, as time progressed, I learned something new about peace, surrender, acceptance, love—me.

In the central thread of every encounter was my own identity. Slightly embarrassed to admit that at 46 years old I am still accepting myself. *Don't you already know who you are? Who continues to re-invent themselves at 46? Get somewhere and sit down. Your time has passed.* The voice of my inner critic is loud. But my will, though more quiet and subtle whispers: Keep going Tamia. You are doing alright. Keep dreaming. Keep growing. Keep learning and unraveling. *Keep remembering and reinventing who you are.* And to that quiet constant voice, I say: I hear you and know you well. You spoke to me as a child of 6 and 9 the same way you did at 16 and 26 and now 46. I remember you. I remember me.

What sense have I made of these events that have occurred now throughout these 46 years? The sense is that I have always been who I am and who I need to be. If I am going to step out in this world and make a significant impact-and I do intend to do just that-I must know myself. The journey is for my own remembrance to come back to myself, my whole complete essence. This journey includes my fears and insecurities, uncertainties and criticisms. It includes my personal belief system and skills, my enjoyments and my talents. It includes my family networks and relationships, my chosen and inherited families. It includes society and its mandates and decisions, the collective reality of all of our power struggles and humanity. It includes my personal agency and the collective agency of the beautiful melanin rich community that I have been placed in. It includes this beautiful mind of mine that I now see—this mind as well.

APPENDIX A:
EATING FOR WELLNESS
MY PLANT BASED LIFE

These are some of the recommended foods according to *The British Journal of Psychiatry*:

Natural Anti-depressants that contain the phytochemical *quercetin*: kale, apples, berries, grapes, onions, green tea.

Alpha Linolenic Acid (ALA) containing foods that the body converts into EPA & DHA the Healthy Fats: Walnuts, Flax Seeds, Chia Seeds, Leafy Green Vegetables.

Amino Acid (Tryptophan) containing foods that the brain uses to produce Serotonin (feelings of happiness & well-being): Leafy Greens, Soybean*, Mushrooms, Broccoli, Peas, Sunflower Seeds, Watercress, Pumpkin Seeds.

Complex Carbohydrate Plant Proteins: vegetable, fruits, whole grains, legumes.

*Fruit and Vegetables rich in anti-oxidants and polyphenols**: oranges, apples, grapes, peaches, grapefruit juice, cherries, blueberries, pomegranate juice, raspberries, cranberries, black elderberries, blackcurrants, plums, blackberries, strawberries, apricots, spinach, onions, shallots, potatoes, black and green olives, globe artichoke heads, broccoli, asparagus, carrots.

Fibroid Elimination Food List*
Black mulberry juice, elderberries, arugula, avocados, black mission figs, black/purple seeded grapes, black cherries, BOK CHOY, burdock,

CALLALLOO/AMARANTH, coconut, dandelion, GREEN BANANAS, HEMP, IRISH SEA MOSS, kelp, kiwi, mango, PAK CHOY, pineapple, wild yam, blood oranges, camu camu, ginger, lemon, lime/key lime.

Various teas, beverages, spices & herbs
Fennel, ginger, peppermint, jasmine, turmeric tea, turmeric nut milk, lemon, chamomile, lavender, hibiscus, warm apple cider, holy basil.

Basil, cilantro, thyme, black salt, pink Himalayan salt, sea salt, onion power, cayenne power, black pepper, garlic cloves, shallots, parsley, rosemary, oregano, cumin, coriander, cardamon.

Apple ginger carrot juice (fresh squeezed or pressed).

Lemon, cucumber, celery juice (fresh squeezed or pressed).

Orange pineapple banana juice (fresh squeezed or pressed).

Peach juice (fresh squeezed or pressed).

Disclaimer: This is not medical or mental health advice or an exhaustive list. One should always consult with their doctor, dietician, or nutritionist when switching meal plans and tune in to how they feel when eating certain things. These are all meals and ingredients I have consumed that helped me in some way.

APPENDIX B:
DEVELOPING YOUR ACTION PLAN FOR SUSTAINABILITY

Developing Your Action Plan for Sustainability: Practical Steps

1. What can you continue, add, adjust or let go?

2. What do you need to learn, maintain, or accept?

3. What will you embrace, allow, reject, or understand?

4. How often will you commit to giving back to yourself?

5. Who will hold you accountable?

Community

Practical Adjustments

Meals & Movement for Resilience

Steps for sustainability

Yoga, Breathing, & Mindfulness

Outlook & Mindset Shift

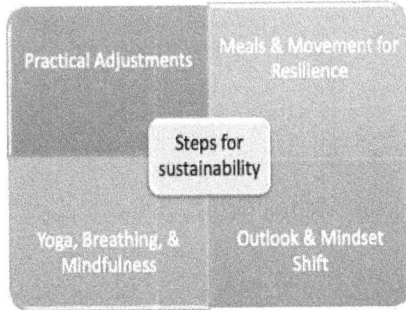

McEwen, Tamia A., (2020) PhD Mind as Well: Living Yoga for Mental and Physical Wellness. Samyama Study Group

APPENDIX C:
SELF CARE ACTION PLAN EXAMPLE

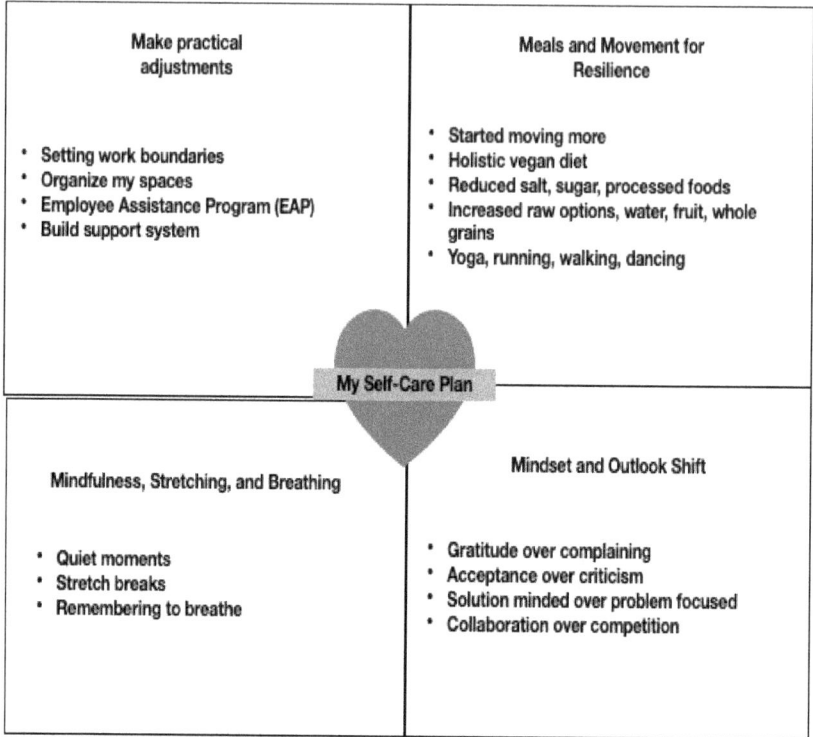

APPENDIX D:
TRANSFORMATION OF MINDSET: BECOMING & UNBECOMING

Transformation of Mindset: Becoming & Unbecoming

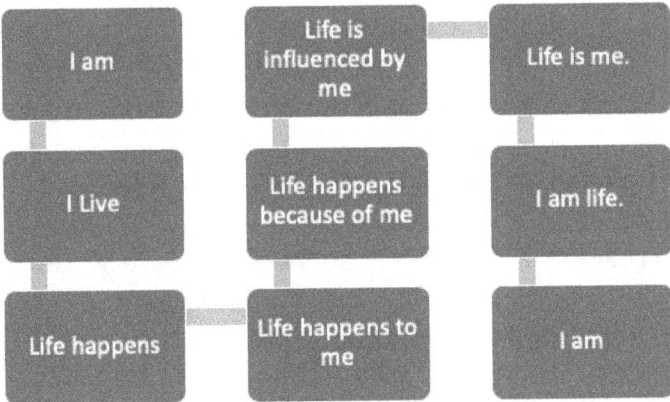

I am	Life is influenced by me	Life is me.
I Live	Life happens because of me	I am life.
Life happens	Life happens to me	I am

McEwen, Tamra A. (2020) PhD Mind to Well-Living Yoga for Mental and Physical Wellness. Sankyama Study Group.

APPENDIX E:
RECOMMENDED READING & RESOURCES

Anpu, A., & Amun, N. (2015). Got Fibroids? The fibroid

elimination bible. Atlanta, GA: LuLu.com.

Arewa, C. S. (2018). Opening to Spirit: Contacting the Healing

Power of the Chakras & Honoring African Spirituality.

Hammersmith, London: Inner Vision Books.

DeGruy Leary PhD, J. (2005). Post Traumatic Slave Syndrome.

Oregon, Milwaukee: Uptone Press.

Garcia, H., & Miralles, F. (2016). Ikigai: The Japanese Secret to

a Long and Happy Life. (H. Cleary, Trans.) New York,

New York: Penguin Books.

Ketabi, S. R. (2017). Ayurveda: Idiot's Guide. Indiannapolis,

Indiana: Mike Sanders.

Korn, L. E. (2016). Nutrition Essential for Mental Health: A

Complete Guide to the Food Mood Connection. New

York: Norton.

Lynch, B. (2018). Dirty Genes: A Breakthrough Program to Treat the Root Cause of Illness and Optimize Your Health New York, New York: HarperOne.

McEwen, T. A. (2019). Mind as Well: A Peer's Perspective of Living Yoga On and Off the Mat. Samyama Study Group. Vero Beach: MacBeWell.

McEwen, T. A. (2020, January 15). Corona Reflections. Retrieved from Be Well Friends, LLC Virtual Wellness Community: www.macbewell.com

Naidoo, U. (2020). *This is your brain on food: An indispensable guide to the surprising foods that fight depression, anxiety, PTSD, OCD, ADHD, and more.*

Patanjali. (2020). The Yoga Sutras. Bibliotech Press.

PCRM.org. (2015). Food and Mood: Eating Plants to Fight the Blues. Washington, DC: Physicians Committee for Responsible Medicine.

Robert Word Johnson Foundation. (2020, January 5). What is Health Equity? Retrieved from www.rwjf.org

Van der Kolk, B. A. (2015). The Body Keeps the Score: Brain,

mind, and body in the healing of trauma. New York,

New York: Penguin Books, Random House

*For additional resources subscribe to www.macbewell.com for

digital update.

Dr. Tamia A. McEwen developed her framework *Lifestyle as Wellness Support (L.A.W.S.)* and employs it when working with individuals and groups. L.A.W.S. is her integrative model that includes health, nutritional psychiatry, and mindfulness. She developed her model because of a fundamental belief: *It's through caring for ourselves that we can collectively care for each other and create a culture of well-being.* She helps individuals and groups develop *cultures of well-being.*

Dr. McEwen's L.A.W.S. model has several components: (i) Taking A P.A.U.S.E. and (ii) Transformation of Mindset & Transformation of Well-being. In today's "new normal," we're constantly trying to "keep up" and "make things happen." She notes that if we're not careful, we'll "burn out" quickly, and our groups and communities will splinter. To avoid that, she helps her clients "hold space" so they can maintain a dynamic equilibrium where forces bind rather than undermine. She holds "space" for herself as well so that she can give from her overflow. **Her** clients include individuals, groups, and organizations of all types.

She received her Doctorate in Curriculum & Instruction (C&I), Texas A&M University, Urban Education, and her Master of Arts (M.A.) in Secondary Reading, Grand Canyon University, and BS in Psychology, Prairie View A&M University. She has received a 200-hour Yoga & Wellness Certification (Breathe for Change), and designations for Level 1 Qigong and Y12SR Space Holder.

Dr. McEwen made her debut as a published author of *Mind as Well: Journey from discovery to recovery and beyond*, which released in 2021. She is the owner of Be Well Friends, L.L.C., virtual wellness community; a board member of Peer Support Coalition of Florida (P.S.C.F.L.), and founder of Treasure Coast Peer Network.

Dr. McEwen partners as a daily Peer facilitator and monthly co-facilitator of Your Black Matters virtual Peer Support. She currently resides in Vero Beach, Florida. For more information, access more information www.macbewell.com or admin@macbewell.com.

MESSAGE OF HOPE

I want to share a message of hope for anyone reading this. Know that you are loved, valued, and worthy of life. You belong here. The words in this book are from my lived experiences and are not to be taken as advice or any roadmap. If you or a someone you know is experiencing a mental health crisis or need someone to talk to, please reach out to a trusted friend, family member, or community member. This crisis hotline is also here for your wellness resource. We are rooting for you!

Love,

Tamia

YOUR FEELINGS ARE VALID.

NEED SUPPORT?
TEXT HOME TO 741741 FOR FREE,
24/7 CRISIS COUNSELING. WE'RE
HERE FOR YOU.

Crisistextline.org